# The South American Diaries

BY THE SAME AUTHOR:

*The Attempt,* The Viking Press, New York, 1967
*Tangier Buzzless Flies,* Athenaeum, New York, 1972
*The Flight of the Pelican,* North Point Press, San Francisco, 1984
*In the Chinese Mountains,* Peter Owen, London, 1990
*Rendez-vous ultimes,* La Table Ronde, Paris 1991
*The Tangier Diaries,* Cadmus Editions, San Francisco, 1998
*All I Wanted Was Company,* Arcadia Books, London, 1999

John Hopkins

# The South American Diaries

(1972-1973)

Cadmus Editions
San Francisco

E-mail: *jeffcadmus@aol.com*
*www.cadmuseditions.com*



Printed in the United States of America

First published by Quai Voltaire, Paris, 2005

**First American Edition**

Hopkins, John L., 1938-
Library of Congress Control Number 2005925794
ISBN 0-932274-68-4 *(trade edition)*
ISBN 0-932274-69-2 *(signed limited edition)*

10 9 8 7 6 5 4 3 2 1

*". . . real adventures . . . do not happen to people who remain at home; they must be sought abroad."*

—James Joyce

*October 6, Guaymas*
*Morning*

On the train from Mexicali to Empalme ($35.00 first-class sleeper for two), suffering from a delicious case of the hangover hots.

We have just finished breakfast in this rattling old American dining car. Huevos fritos with guacamole, refried beans, warm soft tortillas, black coffee and orange juice that I have had to lace with a shot of white rum to stir the tequila blues from last night's excesses.

Beside me, my travelling companion, Madeleine van Breugel, already coifed and made-up, Hermès scarf knotted loosely around her neck, dolled-up like she's going to a party, decked out in expensive jewelry I tell her not to wear south of the border.

Her face-framing mane of just-brushed auburn hair—that's where I should be snuggling, on her shoulder, in that fragrant nest. But I am not snuggling, because another is snuggling there—Chula, the miniature green parrot I bought for her in Guatemala two years ago. That's where he snuggles, and where he has been smuggled, under her hair, past many a customs inspector from JFK to Marrakesh.

Each time I draw near, to give my sweetheart a peck on the cheek, the little nipper emerges from the veil of hair to defend his lair, to return my affection peck for peck. And he has a nasty bite.

Now moving swiftly southwards through thorn and cactus country—cattle country—towards real heat and, perhaps, renewed creativity. Black vultures in the tree-tops . . . the sight of their hunched black forms fills me with nameless desire . . .

We have checked into the Hotel Miramar, reputedly the second best in town, and soon found it is a distant second. Two beds for $20.80. We pushed them together. Lizards roam the room, big ones. They chase the roaches. Not much of a beach and no waves, and the beach is fenced off due to shark fear.

Sunset. The saguaro or sentinel cactus stands tall and solitary, not like the others. They prefer high rocky ground and ridge crests, where they are seen darkly silhouetted against the evening sky. My eye is drawn to these erect sentinels who keep lonely vigil over arid lands, as my spirit is in thrall to the perfect stillness of the desert scene.

In the distance across the water, a row of pointy, spire-like mountains, aptly named *Cerro Tetas de Cabra* (Goat Tits Mountains).

Painted Mexican boys lounging in the Bar Sonora, the pool hall cantina across the street from the hotel, are drunk on beer at eleven o'clock in the morning. They have dyed their hair orange, have curled it, have had their ears pierced and inserted large, gold, dangly earrings, and assume the languid poses of a geisha. We seem to have landed on the "skid row" of Guaymas.

Part of the dialogue from the bar: "Say, those men grabbed that fellow . . . did you see that? Just as he was about to go out the door. There—they're hitting him. Why? Is it fair—so many against one man? But look, he's giving it back—caught one of the coppers right on the chops and sent him sprawling. Oh dear, guns now. Ow! don't do that! Right across the face with the gun barrel and down he goes . . . they're kicking him. Blood—who's going to be next? Keep your paws off me, you dirty old man! Don't you see what they're doing?"

Limes pressed against my teeth explode juice into my mouth. Never a hangover from tequila? Dehydration from alcohol. The large quantity of salt taken with excessive shots of tequila conserves the moisture in the body. Tequila, I have learned, brings on fears, bad dreams, paranoia.

The democracy of the Mexican cantinas, the loud-mouthed democracy. What knocks it all to pieces—our Yankee habit of saving or investing money—is that down here in Mexico the men, instead of handing it over to their women, blow it in bars, loan it to their friends, fork it over to pimps and whores. They deny the money-saving capitalist instinct.

*October 7. Still in Guaymas*

The ferry to Santa Rosalilla has been delayed by a cyclone which blew up last night and smashed some fishing boats on the beach at the Miramar, so we are obliged to stay one more day in this one-horse town.

The crickets. Our room is full of them, making a screeching and rumbling racket like miniature machines in need of an oiling. The parrot is afraid of them and begins to shout. The Mexican baby in the next room sets up a howl, etc.

Yaqui Indian words:
*tutuli ousi* = beautiful thing, e.g.
a young boy or girl or a jewel
*tobi* = money
*moni* = tortilla
*taishka* = beans
*chinchorro* = large net
*naraya* = small hand net
*pitaya* = bunch cactus
*saguaro* = sentinel cactus
*alcatraz* = pelican (must derive from the Arabic)
*xopilote* = vulture

I am counting on myself to harden up on this trip, to begin to live strenuously and romantically again, to trim excess fat from mind and body.

Even before the publication of my novel *Tangier Buzzless Flies* in February, I had completed the first draft of a new work, provisionally entitled *Xenophobic Dogs*. Set in South America, the work annoys and disappoints me, one of the reasons being I feel I have lost touch with the Latin scene and need to reacquaint myself.

So Madeleine and I have left La Petite Maison—our adobe house in the palm groves outside Marrakesh where we have been living for the past year and a half—rented it while we travel and live in South America. My ultimate aim for this trip is to hole up in some tropical port town long enough to bang out a final draft of this novel that is burning a hole in my briefcase.

Although we set out with high expectations, the trip is already fraught with uncertainty. Madeleine, separated from her husband but not divorced, has a four-year-old daughter, Julie, back in Holland she feels desperately guilty about leaving. On top of this her favorite uncle Daan Hubrecht, at whose house in Tangier we met, is seriously ill with cancer. Madeleine has promised she will return immediately if his condition deteriorates . . . so this trip may be over before we know it, and we don't even have a house to live in.

*October 8, 4:15 PM*

On board the ferry *Presidente Díaz Ordaz* ($13.60) from Guaymas, Sonora, to Santa Rosalilla, Baja California.

So, at last, the Sea of Cortez—Steinbeck's sea—peaceful and blue. We have just awoken from a deep siesta into which I inevitably fall south of the border. Like Lima all over again—the irresistible siesta.

There are musicians in the first class bar, and dancing, and Mexicans becoming drunker and drunker . . .

Ah! The unbroken horizon, the sea like a great blue disc, the tropical sea! Following seagulls. I was sitting on deck reading Malcolm Lowry's *Letters* when a huge whale breached off the stern of the ship!

Pound called the sea: "The Whale's Acre."

We have seen Arab profiles among the Mexicans, not surprising when you consider that many of the early conquistadors came from Estremadura, one of the poorest provinces of Spain, where Islamic customs lingered long after the Moors were expelled. They were Mohammedans only recently Christianized, which may explain their religious fanaticism, their habit of cutting throats, bringing their Moorish physiognomies with them to South America.

*October 9, Muleje, Baja California. Taxi Hotel Casitas $16.00*

Dawn. Pelicans. The peace of these waters. The pelicans stand on lines of rotted pilings. One pelican silhouette to a piling. Pelicans and pilings welded together against the fiery yellow water of sunrise.

She cried herself to sleep last night. I want her to sleep some more, so I have slipped from beneath the mosquito netting, carried my notebook onto the terrace, and now sip coffee in my underwear, mull over last night's event and those that have brought us here, and am consoled, a little, by the appearance of my favorite bird.

The pelican floating upon the water has not the sleek profile of the gull or duck. The humped wing shoulders and arched neck, with a bill so long that the tip is not held out of the water, give the impression of top-heaviness. The bird in flight, however, surpasses the others in gliding power. With a wingspan so broad it has only to flap a few times to sail a long distance, low over the water, wing tips just missing the swinging wave ends. You see them flying home in the evening, a long line of them, in ragged V formation, etched against the pink cumulus on the horizon. The whole flock will flap together and glide low over the undulating sea tables, like a formation of heavy bombers. Superbly designed for the air, they land, webbed feet down and wide apart with a sliding splash, keeping the wings high and dry. Taking off, they appear heavily laden, and kick the water to get air-borne. An awkward configuration specifically designed for gliding. A bird so clumsy in appearance, so graceful in the air. I must watch them. Their long bills make neat movements. And they are reckless divers.

She got through to Holland last night. An only daughter, Madeleine used to be her father's favorite, but now he refuses to speak to her, except to say she'll never be welcome under the family roof again. Her mother came on the phone to say that Madeleine's husband has taken their daughter to France, but she wouldn't say where, or how to get in touch with them.

*October 10, La Paz, Baja California. Hotel La Perla $32.00*

Arrived here by dusty desert bus from Muleje. When you travel with a good-looking woman south of the border, you get all kinds of offers—free food, free rides, especially free drinks—which initially flatter and deceive, until you realize it's got nothing to do with you. It's her they're after. They're trying to get past you to her. It's her they want to get close to. They want you to get drunk or lost, so you can't defend her.

*October 11*

At 6 AM the sun rises like a flare jutting into the sky. I awoke blinded by the sun and covered with a greasy patina of perspiration that won't evaporate till sundown. Still reeling from last night's excesses, I staggered onto the balcony to look at the sea.

Black skimmers or *dijeretas*. These black (the mature ones have white breasts) pterodactyl-like birds, which we first saw in Guatemala, have long tapering, incredibly thin arched wings. Like vultures they soar to great heights, so great that one wonders what they could be doing up there. Narrow, swallow tail. Long beak with a hook at the end of it. Fragile wings that resemble umbrella material. Here, sitting on the 3rd-floor veranda of the Hotel Perla, overlooking the bay in front of the city (whose shoddy "duty-free" shops remind me of Las Palmas in the Canary Islands), I can observe them at eye-level as they glide over the palm-tops just a few yards away. And, through my binoculars I can watch them enter into swirling dog fights with the vultures, at tremendous altitudes. They do not dive into the water like the pelican, who always beats them to a fish, but gather their prey by skimming the surface of the sea, beak open.

Last night during a romantic, hand-holding dinner beneath the palms at Las Brisas restaurant on the beach—cold white wine from California and *cabrilla,* a small but delicious fish, firm flesh with the consistency of swordfish and San Pedro (John Dory) combined, *a la parilla*—we decided that Paramaribo in Surinam, formerly Dutch Guiana in northeast South America, the city of mahogany, will be our destination. We'll rent a shack on the beach, and I'll get down to work on the novel. As Surinam is a former Dutch colony, communication with Holland should be easy. Should she get the call, Madeleine can fly home from there.

So we will set off for Mexico City, not knowing exactly how we will proceed from there. But who knows in Veracruz there might be a Dutch freighter with an empty cabin, next port of call Surinam . . .

After that love-confirming dinner we made the mistake of stopping off at Cantina Misión for a night-cap before going to bed.

As soon as we got inside the door we were accosted by a Mexican who insisted on buying us drink after drink with the intention of seeing what we (mostly Madeleine) would do when we got drunk. Horrible feeling of being trapped, not by the Mexican, for we could have walked out of there any time (the bar, located beneath the hotel, had no windows, adding perhaps to the sense of claustrophobia), but trapped by our idiotic ignorance of the Mexican's intentions, which became abundantly clear afterwards.

Madeleine, ever the exhibitionist, danced her hip-gyrating, hand-on-butt Swazi dance to the mariachi musicians, also hired by the same calculating Mexican. She was invited to sit down by other men at their tables, which she refused to do. The slimy Mexican, nevertheless, insisted on rescuing her from them, and dancing with her. All the while I sat at the bar listening to some red-neck American here on a fishing trip, a friend of the Mexican, rant on about *work* and the *coloreds*.

Taking out my pocket watch, I looked at the time. A minute later, realizing that I had looked at the watch face without the hour registering in my head, I took out the watch again . . . this is what tequila does.

Finally we made it out of there, came back to the room where I scolded her for that sexy dance which made the Mexicans as crazy as wildcats.

In the Parade Bar in Tangier she used to perform the same dance, with the parrot sitting on her head, to the Jilala or Gnaoua beat. To some she made a fool out of herself; others thought her dance was sensational.

I was jealous then and I'm jealous and angry now over the raw male attention the dance provokes. But my words bounce off with no effect. It's like she's wearing a suit of armor . . . only a few sparks . . . and a resentful fire from those gray-green eyes.

Jealousy, I say, "Just because you think you haven't experienced it, don't pretend it doesn't exist!"

Chin in the air she turns away. My jealousy infringes on her impulse to dance whenever she damn well feels like it.

*October 12*

We share our room with a pelican with a broken wing. She rescued it from the beach where it was menaced by pariahs. Takes up the whole bathroom. She feeds it dead fish. One hell of a mess . . . shits all over the place. The smell. A powerful bird, even in its enfeebled state. Claws for toes. She wants to take it with us, but I say look, with the mountain of luggage we've already got, I can't handle travelling with a bird with a five-foot wing spread. Luckily, she's found a kindred soul in the bartender, an animal lover who says he'll take it off our hands when we leave town.

*October 13*

On board the ferry *La Paz* bound for Mazatlán. The joy upon discovering that you have been assigned a spacious comfortable cabin with two portholes. ($48 first class for two.) Gulping sea air by the ship's rail makes us sane again.

The snowman. Enormous, powerful, with a bulging paunch, he never seems to sweat, even in this heat. Dressed from head to toe in white. Ubiquitous—he's the head steward, bartender, takes and gives orders in the restaurant, changes money and, for all I know, pilots the ship. When we step from our cabin, he's always there—cool, mountainous, billowing white as he bows. "You want something, sir?" We feel he's stalking us and take evasive action. He joshes with the young crew members, but we can see they're scared of him. Evidently a predatory homosexual.

*October 14, Mazatlán. Hotel Belmar $8.40*
*Mariscos Restaurant Mamuca*

Tequila plus salt air makes me dream like mad. Last night, on the boat, a long conversation in a café with a gentle, balding Albert Camus. I said, "I thought you were dead, killed in that car crash in France." He said, "No, I live in Moscow now . . . " and smiled apologetically, enigmatically.

Mazatlán—a sloppy, tropical seaport . . . looks like plenty of good times here. While Madeleine and Chula napped, I headed down to the seafront for a swim. Mammoth, smoking Pacific combers crunched on the steep beach. Hades-hot, but no one was in swimming. One step into the water told me why. A heavy undertow nearly yanked my feet out from under me. A warning from the water. This ocean is not to be fooled with. I abandoned my plan to body-surf and splashed around in the shallow water before hopping barefoot through the sizzling streets back to the hotel. A quick stop in a cantina for liquid refreshment. I think this lime juice is eroding the enamel off my teeth.

On the beach at Mazatlán they call it:

*leño*
*carrujo*
*grifa*
*mota (ita)*

*suspira*
*saumbido*
*toque*

The overhead fan beats out an insistent rhythm above the languid form of the sleeping girl. This tequila! Almost too weak to pick up the suitcases now. They take up half the room in this zero-star hotel. How did we accumulate so many? Madeleine's "face box" containing her "war paint," her jewelry box, and the Moroccan basket with tight-fitting lid that is Chula's travel-house. Two huge suitcases full of expensive clothes, enough to go around the world in. But she's not the only one. My leather case crammed with medicine for asthma, malaria, Montezuma's revenge, plus Bandaids, syringes, bugbomb and four heavy, ledger-like notebooks bought at the Princeton U-Store to record this diary in. My ten-year-old but still serviceable Spanish briefcase holds the first draft of *Xenophobic Dogs,* which I've barely looked at. The hockey puck I use as a paperweight. The portable Smith Corona. My Swiss army knife. This ancient leather suitcase my father gave me weighs a ton even when empty. Why did I bring so many clothes when all I've worn so far are khakis, shirt, sandals and straw hat? Why did I buy this suit, not even a summer suit, at Saks in New York when I'll probably never wear it? Plus assorted baskets full of souvenirs and shopping, food for Chula, a bag full of sea shells and pelican bones I collected off the beaches of Baja—fourteen in all.

Also a sackful of books: Gide's *The Immoralist (c'est moi)*. Bernal Díaz—*The Betrayal of Montezuma. History of the Conquest of Peru* by W. H. Prescott. *Lost Trails, Lost Cities* by Col. P. Fawcett. Carlos Castaneda—*The Journey to Ixtlán. The Raw and the Cooked* by Claude Lévi-Strauss. *The Sea and the Jungle* by H. M. Tomlinson. *Travel and Adventure in Many Lands* by Cecil Gosling, etc.

*October 15*

On the train from Mazatlán to Mexico City, via Guadalajara. The name of our car is *Marruecos* (Morocco in Spanish). What a weird coincidence. What does it mean? Lowry would make something of this.

I feel heavy inside . . . the head isn't working too well . . . got to lay off the tequila. Going through the motions of maintaining this journal, feeling the darkness within. One problem is—I can never tell whether she's happy or not. Perhaps we have jumped beyond that simple consideration. If so, I'm not sure where we've landed. The constant preoccupations, the mood swings she refuses to discuss. Emotions become dangerous when you don't deal with them.

The truth of the matter is that I'll probably never be able to make her happy because we've sinned. A sin that can never by atoned for, explained away, or assuaged by the passage of time. She left her husband and ran off with me. Worse, much worse, she left her child behind. She's been ostracized by her family. That's more emotional baggage than we can lift. We live with pain we cannot escape, no matter how far we run. She says, *"Sabes todo,"* which means she loves me, but is love worth this amount of suffering, our flawed and imperfect love?

But, boarding the train, we both somehow begin to feel better. She's laughing at Chula flying around inside the compartment, shitting here and there.

What is it about the road? Why do I always feel lighter when I'm on it? Movement seems to loosen my brain. The rocking of this train dislodges fresh ideas from the crannies of my mind. Shifting vistas evoke deeper meanings. Rimbaud tramped all over Europe with a head full of visions. He was a hard man, road-toughened. It's my bet he got all his ideas on the road. Only a hobo understands this feeling of liberation. I can see right now that this journal will be my salvation until I get to work on the novel. I've just got to keep on writing things down.

We have locked up the parrot, opened the window and lean out, excited, as the train chugs along.

Cane fields, green hills and red earth. Children with shiny brown bodies splash like seals in brown rivers. Men on horseback and astride donkeys, with machetes. A profusion of orange flowers, the dark morning glory, broad flats of the water hyacinth. The ubiquitous vultures circle. Extinct green volcanoes . . . others, with clouds of steam pouring out. Gigantic thunderheads build up in the afternoon. We have climbed up from the coast, and the air is cooler, drier. Multiple slumped volcanoes. The hazy peaks of the Sierra Madre Occidental in the distance, where Humphrey Bogart sweated for gold. No, wrong, as he set out from Tampico, he would have panned for gold in the eastern range. B. Traven knew his way around. Gila monster country, jaws like steel. They say the lizard won't release its grip until the sun goes down. You have to chop its head off. Actually their bites aren't poisonous . . . they just chew into you the regurgitated contents of their last putrid meal.

Suddenly, it's much darker. Thunderheads have blotted out the sun. Banana farms, sisal plantations, these bright green hills. The blue-gray sisal is planted along hillsides in wavy rows. An ancient lava flow. Madeleine points out a cloud like a ragged fish swimming past an exhausted mountain. Mountains have spewed out other mountains, ridges and hills—the whole configuration of the landscape vomited from the giant's maw. Corn grows everywhere—in the valleys and on hillsides so steep they only could have been tilled by the Indian hand plough. A fiery sunset—great glittering streaks of yellow light falling behind us in the west. Volcanoes do brood over a landscape. Circling vultures do cast a spell . . .

Malcolm Lowry's *Letters*—after the publication of *Volcano*, the tension seems to have gone out.

*October 16, Mexico City. Hotel Maria Cristina $74.00*
*Restaurant (Mariscos) Colonial Laredo*

High, cold and gray. Dizziness in the head, weakness in the limbs, especially the arms. The suitcases have become as heavy as lead. After the languid beach life of Baja, the swirl and noise of this big city confuses us. Altitude sickness? Difficulty in hearing, remembering, even caring. Or the result of too much tequila? Unaccountable lack of concentration, difficulty in keeping any thought in front of the mind. Fatigue—can't walk, diminished appetite.

The first thing I did when we arrived in Mexico City, even before we had left the railroad station, was to buy a train ticket out of here.

A few drops of rain come down and the electricity shuts off. Street transformers erupt in green flame as the citizens run for their lives. Ah well, a city of ten million Mexicans has to be one crazy place. A miracle anything works, and, at eight thousand feet, no wonder one feels out of joint. This morning Madeleine was very nearly run down by a fleet of charging, roaring, polluting second-hand taxis imported from the United States. *Very nearly.* The horror and the absurdity of that. The wide boulevards: one minute they're empty, the next seething with these decrepit stock cars which have been given a green flag at an intersection around the corner, bearing down on one. After yanking her back, we clung to each other as the herd of wheeled machines thundered by.

Suave, good-looking, Spanish-speaking German businessmen in continental suits stride confidently before ranks of jewelry shops. Every other store sells either optical equipment or shoes.

And, to top it all off, we had to choose a vegetarian restaurant, where they served up this weird food . . . And God, what dreams! They torture me . . . every . . . single . . . night. Must be the tequila.

*The dream:*

M and I visit Paul Bowles, who is the guardian of a lighthouse, a small one. He lives with a nasty woman and her son, an enormous 17-year-old, who says little but gives everyone dirty looks. Very bad vibrations from this scene. We are very ill at ease. Finally they set off in a car towing a trailer as big as a house. (In fact it is their house on wheels; M and I are to live in a hut.) Somehow, we do accompany them, along dusty roads. Paul very much harassed by the woman and her son.

We arrive at a crossroads, where Paul, M and I are separated from the others. The locale suddenly is Far Hills, NJ, and I plead with Paul to come with us to my mother's house, where he will be free from the woman. But Paul as usual is nervous, indecisive, weak. It becomes clear that we'll never be able to get him away, although he is clearly being abused and taken advantage of by the woman and her son.

Then down the dusty road ambles Jane. We all meet, the six of us, at the crossroads.

Final scene: Jane is a school teacher, sitting at a desk, paying no attention to her students, as she counts, over and over again, a pile of traveler's checks. The checks are bent and wrinkled in her hands. The class is in chaos. The children chant that Jane is a "tattletale."

*October 17, Mexico City*

The noise, the traffic, the fumes. One is dependent on taxi drivers, who churlishly demand insane prices, then get lost, or never knew where they were going in the first place.

A hangover doesn't help. But the day has turned sunny, I have the train tickets to Tapachula on the border with Guatemala in my pocket, and we are relaxing in our room at the pleasant Maria Cristina. Found in a local bookstore a copy of *Under the Volcano*, so I can put down *October Ferry*, which for some reason irritates me. And, for Madeleine, *Green Mansions* by W. H. Hudson.

*October 18*

My God, I was depressed this morning—shaky, and with a stone in my heart. Last night she announced that she had had enough of this aimless, airless, booze-fuelled trip, and that she was leaving—all forgotten, apparently, this morning. When the distance wells up between us, and we are like strangers lying side by side in bed, without touching, with little in common, with nothing to say, I feel sick, I cannot stand it. And alcohol makes everything so much worse.

But, thank God, things seem better now. We've spent a happy afternoon gazing at Aztec treasures in the archaeological museum, and the train tickets out of here tomorrow are in my pocket.

When you think of what that Indian civilization created here in Mexico City . . . "the great Montezuma descended from his litter, and these other great *caciques* supported him beneath a marvellously rich canopy of green feathers, decorated with goldwork, silver, pearls, and *chalchihuites* which hung from a sort of border. It was a marvellous sight. The great Montezuma was magnificently clad, in their fashion, and wore sandals of a kind for which their name is *cotaras,* the soles of which are gold and the upper parts ornamented with precious stones." —*The Betrayal of Montezuma* by Bernal Díaz.

. . . and when you see what's here now . . . Brion Gysin may have had a point after all. The human race has fouled its nest. The point is to get off this planet p.d.q. and start up again some place else.

The doomed prince fashioned his crown of the Quetzal. And so doomed the bird.

*October 20, Veracruz*

On the train from Mexico City to Tapachula, Chiapas ($18.40), waiting in the train station in Veracruz, the train being some three hours late to depart.

Some say that forms of worship are influenced by the environment. Our fate is presently controlled by the *porteros,* engineers, and conductors of the *Ferrocarriles Nacionales de Mexico.* To the latter we are obliged to pay homage in the form of small bribes so that Chula may ride with us in the *Carro Dormitorio* and not be consigned to the dreary solitude of the mail car.

Last night we left high Mexico City and, after a hectic night (many jerking starts and abrupt screeching halts, as if the engineer was trying to avoid numerous small animals crossing the tracks), I raised the window shade this morning to behold palm trees, dark forested hills wreathed in mist, thatch huts, red roads, and men on horseback, armed with machetes. We have providentially brought along a basket of food and drink (purchased yesterday in the formidable La Merced market), for this train has *ni comedor ni bar,* and we have—at least—24 hours of travel ahead of us.

What with her love of cooking and interest in exotic food, Madeleine sprang to life at La Merced market. A hall the area of an airplane hangar full of avocados, ranging from pitless ones the size and shape of Seville oranges to monsters you could mistake for watermelons. Piles of red and orange mangoes. (How my love loves mangoes!) We bought a basketful of those. Best of all, in between the stalls, cantinas serving ice-cold margaritas and ceviche at 11.30 in the morning. Baskets bulging, we staggered out of there, happily plastered.

And last night, while I lay in the upper bunk reading, and Chula gnawed a mango pit, she prepared tacos in our rocking compartment. Like her pet bird, she's happiest when making a nest . . .

Having just finished Lowry's letters, in particular that 40-page impassioned plea to his agent in New York, Harold Matson, now my agent—his son Peter Matson—I began re-reading last night, with intense pleasure and fresh comprehension, *Under the Volcano*. The beleaguered novelist in a far-off land, with only his vision to convince, only the muse for companionship, and, in Lowry's case, the bottle—this lethal, local hooch.

Yep, I am now sipping *Mezcal con Gusano.* Monte Alban brand. *Regional de Ouaxaca. Hecho en Mexico.* The bottle containing the golden nectar is touchingly embossed with Aztec pyramids, solemn ceremonial masks, war club, rattlesnakes, cacti, a metate, and the agave plant from which the alcohol is fermented—visions, I suppose, Mexicans see when they gulp this firewater. The segmented, cylindrical agave worm cruises like a miniature submarine at the bottom of the bottle. While staring at the embalmed beast, an idea springs from the juice: I'll call my seedy South American port town Puerto Gusano in the novel. Worm Hole. It's perfect. Worm Hole by Night.

Lesson for the day: While breakfasting in the grimy restaurant of this train station I observed with disgust a huge man—fat, unshaven, stomach bulging unnaturally over his belt (a rope) —stuffing himself with greasy pastry and drinking from a half-gallon bottle of Coca Cola. At that moment he epitomized for me everything that is wasteful, idle, dirty, sloppy, stupid and useless in this country. Fending off the insistent urchins, mendicants and shoeshine boys, I focussed upon this one unsuspecting fellow the sum of my impatience with the railroad company, the incipient nausea brought on by the tepid coffee I was forcing myself to consume, and the nagging dissatisfaction with my inability to make progress on the book. I really hated him then.

This same gentleman, however, has just turned up on the train, peddling guava jelly, which he politely insisted we taste before purchasing, deftly carving off delicate slivers with a pen knife. It was delicious. The man was exceedingly pleasant, exuding an oriental calm which suited his grotesque proportions. Selling us the block of jelly for a few pennies, he courteously wished us a safe journey, his bloated face both gentle and generous in expression.

A bell has just rung loudly. Can it be the signal that we are about to depart? Last night when the train made one of its wrenching, unscheduled stops, I snapped awake and could not go back to sleep until we were underway once more. Now two bells—like a ship will we depart at three? Catching a glimpse from the railroad station restaurant of gleaming white freighters in the port, I longed to unload our baggage from this lurching lizard, and set sail for exotic ports across glittering seas, where the alabaster walls of tropical thunderheads, veined with silent lightning, pile up on the horizon.

A woman on the train is screaming her head off. Unnerving

howls of the deranged . . .

Three bells . . . still we do not move. Finally, at 2.30 PM—five hours late—we pull out. Down the aisle *la loca* is throwing another fit. Name of the first stop: Paso del Toro. Like in an old western movie, we took on water from a big wooden tank with a tube that swings out over the track.

A tiny church, no bigger than an outhouse, has its own cross —two of them, and a miniature bell.

*La loca* has started up again, a deep hollow voice, like the bellowing of a wounded bull. Her friends throw a blanket over her, to muffle the noise. Everything becomes connected now, like the links of a sausage, as *Volcano* begins to cast its spell. What can those savage cries mean? What dimension of agony, that is?

The kudzu vine is devouring this country, too.

The pace of the novel must be as slow, swirling, opaque, and eddying as the muddy Amazon, with its sinuous route toward the mother of rivers, also the death of rivers—the sea.

*Chulascos* = lightning bugs

Dusk. Standing on the open rear platform of this old-fashioned train, as we rattled across the Mexican landscape, I watched their myriad beacons blinking within the darkening forest. Saw-tooth mountains were silhouetted against the yellow mirror of the sky. Miraculous how those gleaming, parallel, ever-receding tracks cleave the encroaching jungle. The last stop: Sweaty Mile, a moniker evidently given by the grimy guys who built this line.

Tragedy requires efficiency of form, precision of content, but most of all, logic of character. Lowry probed his own soul to produce great fiction. It's frightening—the self-destructive tool he used to pry open the truth was alcohol. I wonder if I'll ever know what it means to give 100% of my heart, soul, and time to my writing, as he did. Right now I'm far from it . . .

*October 21. Still on the train*

Now approaching the Guatemalan frontier. Rio Suchiate. A town—El Carmen. More extinct volcanoes, darkly forested. Pigs roam free on dirt roads. Brahma cattle. Oxen drag the thick-wheeled carts through mud and water, down green lanes. The first ceibas—the white-hulled patriarchs of the forest—and a pink ibis.

*Tapachula, Chiapas. Talisman: $3.25 (taxi)*

Back in Guatemala, where we were once happy. Now the first thing I notice are the black bow ties of death. Large crepe paper black bow ties placed over doorways of houses signifying the presence of death within. They obsess me. What does it all mean?

Bridges: *Nil, Besa, Maricón*—imagine calling a bridge a Nothing, a Kiss, a Queer. Many bridges. We're on the bus now (Talisman-Guatemala City $5.00). The polite and daring young bus driver and his charming but exceedingly unhelpful helper, who sits on the arm of the driver's seat all the way to the capital, whispering sweet nothings into his ear, diverting his attention from the road.

*October 22, Guatemala City*
*Hotel Ritz Continental $60.00*

Last time here we stayed in the flea-bag Centro Americano and were happier. The memory of luxury, lacking the sharp edges of discomfort and the challenge to make it better, fades in time to nothing.

The hollow booming of cannons over the city is answered by what sounds like the rasping reports of small arms fire. Has a revolution started? Fingers of silent lightning play between the volcanoes Aqua and Fuego. It is three o'clock in the morning, it is raining in the jungle, and I am writing by flashlight. Her silent suffering builds an invisible wall between us. To be truthful, maybe it's not quite that dramatic. Let's say, not enough body action, even less head work. Sometimes, very often, I just wonder where we are, why are we together, why have we come back here? What I hate most of all is finding myself making up excuses, letting pass without comment the obviously insensitive remarks she uses to get at me, mainly the spiteful jabs about the time I spend writing. And I'm not really writing; I'm just jotting things down. But she's riddled with guilt, and guilt needs a target. Well, I've learned to take the heat, but the result is I feel utterly alone with the thoughts inside my head.

*Morning*

The cannons, in fact, were rockets and the resounding rifle fire strings of firecrackers—so the shoeshine man in the park informed me, as he gave my sandals a brilliant shine—set off by the Indians in the Temple of the Calvary a few blocks away.

Had my picture taken by an Indian photographer with his

ancient wooden tripod apparatus on the corner next to said church where, two-and-a-half years ago, on our first trip to Guatemala, we bought Chula, a.k.a. Chita, who was then working as an apprentice fortune-teller. It's true—you paid the Indian a penny and his pet parrot picked a piece of paper from a pile, with your fortune on it.

And while I was out of the hotel exploring the streets, learning these things and having adventures, Chula escaped through the window and flew in circles over the rooftops of the city and finally back to Madeleine, who was in a panic, still shaking and pale when I returned to the hotel an hour later. She had mobilized the hotel maids who had rushed into the street carrying waste baskets to trap the critter. I don't opine that the little feather duster probably wanted to go home and maybe our sex life would improve if he did.

A view down the street from el Bar Moro where I had my first *aguardiente* of the day: a profusion of stop lights, neon signs, movie theatres, automobiles, motorcycles, slot machine parlors, ending with the green wall of the jungle.

Logic of the event, or the thought behind it, or the emotion of the event(s) preceding it. The freedom I experience sitting in a park in Guatemala City, having my shoes shined, playing slot machines for nickels and dimes in a crowd of gawking street urchins. Am I wrong, or do I sense new characters and a dark plot looming in the background? Like those smoky volcanic smoulderings above Fuego, the streets of this city give me a tingling hint of—what?—sweating cities, foreign languages, *Payaso* (clown) cigarettes, cratered landscapes, volcanoes, loving ten-cent shoeshines, the round timeless Indian faces, and toweringly imminent tropical storms—but mainly, a premonition inspired by the BLACK BOWTIES OF DEATH.

As a writer I feel in a quandary. *Xenophobic Dogs* is not working (to date) because I have failed to move anywhere inside my head since the completion of *Tangier Buzzless Flies.* The adventures of an American in a foreign land—I have done that. But foreign lands—the impoverished ones where nature still dominates—do move me. This is where I learned to write, and I have chosen them as my literary domain. Lowry learned to burrow deep within a man— himself, to his cost—as did Melville, whom he admired. Me—I feel stranded on the surface, a balsa raft, Amazon-bound, without much current, drifting.

A balsa raft floats for a month. Then, water-logged, it begins to sink.

Patrolling the streets of Guatemala City—crowded but clean, comfortable, sunlit and pleasing in their grid-like layout—I sense another presence following parallel alleyways, shadowing me step-for-step but inevitably ducking into a doorway or darting behind a lamppost when I stop and look sharply back. Ahead or behind me, or walking beside me, a new idea lurks. This may sound like fantasy, but I do have hopes. This is known as . . . waiting, desperately . . . for some — any—idea that will further the book along. I am subconsciously willing the story into existence, conjuring up new laws my characters must obey.

*October 23*

Clanky bells mark the hour. (The colonial bells.) How in fact *do* they mark the hour? e.g.: at 8 AM—3 clanks. Now, at 11 AM, 26 clanks, then for good measure 3 more clanks. Cobbled streets, yellow walls. Barred windows spaced far apart. Flowers behind bars.

Last night in the Bar Moro we held a strategy session.

Shall we stop here in Guatemala, a country we've travelled over and come to love? Shall we board the train down to Puerto Barrios, as we did two years ago, take the boat across the bay to Livingston and hole up in that crazy hotel, or, better yet, rent a shack on the edge of the jungle where I can get down to work?

Two years ago, in February, 1970, after a riotous evening at the Hotel Miramar in Livingston (already immortalized as "Nile Town" in *Xenophobic Dogs*), we hired an outboard motor-driven canoe which ferried us up the Rio Dulce to Lake Izabel. For two days we were stranded by torrential rain in the village of El Estor, where we were treated to the local delicacy . . . alligator. Meat as white as chicken breast and for the first nibble or two, it actually seems to taste like chicken—you will it to taste like chicken—only a lot tougher. Bite three, a fishy flavor creeps in, followed by the oily aftertaste—reptile.

From El Estor we hitchhiked to the great Mayan city of Tikal, in the process of being excavated by the University of Pennsylvania. At dusk we climbed the great pyramid. Sitting where Mayan priests once performed human sacrifice, we watched the moon pick its way out of the trees. The mystery of the moonlit jungle—it's not so scary when you're perched above the canopy of the massive ceibas. We listened while the monkeys and the parrots went to sleep, heard their parting calls before they clammed up for the night, giving way to the nocturnal roar of insects.

Then by junglebus (name of bus: *Como Siempre*—Same As Always) to Sayatché on the Rio de la Pasión, where Hector and his dugout canoe awaited us. Along the way an Indian carrying a rifle leapt out of the forest, flagged down the bus, and dragged aboard the carcass of the deer (*veneno*) he had just shot.

Me, ever vigilant about personal comfort and concerned about supplies for the proposed river trip we had prearranged in Antigua (Mad. pleading—"No more alligator!"), I began to bargain with the man over his beast. We agreed on a price, and he unsheathed his machete and butchered the deer right there on the bus. In Sayatché I proudly stepped out with two bloody haunches of venison, delicate pointed hooves joined by palmetto twine.

With Hector, our Indian guide, and Raul, his motorman, we glided down the Pasión in a dugout canoe, camping out the first night at Altar de los Sacrificios, where we explored the ruins. Madeleine was in her element—close to nature, far from the conflicting demands of family and civilization. Crouching by the campfire, she supervised the roasting of the venison while I busied myself with the all-important cocktails. *Aguardiente* and lime juice cooled by a supply of ice I had fortuitously acquired in Sayatché. With the rush of the river in our ears we slept on cots beneath mosquito netting, secure in the company of our guides with their rifles and machetes.

The Pasión joined the broader Usumacinta, and two days later we reached our destination on the Mexican border, the great jungle-choked Mayan city known as Yaxchilan. That night we spent in the "Yaxchilan Hilton" (the words scrawled on a plank over the door of a roach-infested hut); but I never got to see the ruins because the first morning, as I was going down for a swim (the rainy season was just beginning and the river lay deep within its channel), I slipped on the greasy bank, tumbled twenty feet into the water, twisting my right knee, which swelled to the size of a melon. Madeleine, ever resourceful in an emergency, walked into the forest with Hector's machete, and hacked a jungle crutch from the forked branch of a tree. With no painkillers in my medical kit, I spent the rest of the river trip sipping from a bottle of *aguardiente.*

That month (Feb. '70) there was a total eclipse of the sun in Guatemala, which we watched through my knee x-rays (nothing broken, ligaments torn). As the moon inched across the sun, the roosters began to crow, and the cattle and sheep returned from the fields, believing it was nightfall. The phenomenon also confused wild animals; monkeys screeched in the trees and the birds fell silent in the unnatural darkness.

Guatemala was a grand adventure, but now we are eager to explore other places. Madeleine, passive, nursing the pain in her heart, lets me make the decisions. Like me she has a yen to see the mighty Amazon, travel up it by boat from mouth to source, so we have decided to keep moving. Tomorrow we set off once more—San Salvador, Honduras, Nicaragua, Costa Rica, to Panama—via T.I.C.A. *(Transportes Internacionales Centro-Americano)*. $35.00

*October 24, San Salvador, Salvador*
*Gran Hotel $16.50*

Scenes from along the road:
Volcanoes truncated by cloud. Fire and water. Fuego y Agua are their names. Pine forests above Goat City. The meticulously terraced farms. Bougainvillaea brilliant in the high clear sunlight. Flame trees, vultures, wild flowers—yellow and orange. A shrine to Santa Rosa de Lima, far from home. Bananas and coffee growing together—the banana trees provide the shade. Poinsettia—dazzling! Rain, sun. White cows dot the green hills. Handmade crosses along the road mark the places where buses have gone screaming over the cliff. Glint of water through the trees. Indian boys are in swimming. Brown bodies glisten in the sunlight like sleek young otters. Women washing clothes, pounding them on rocks.

Name of next town: Poblano Proximo (Next Town).

Beside the road, a shack: *La Cantina Donde Lloran Los Valientes* (The Bar Where Brave Men Cry).

Two whores in Bermuda shorts—one Brazilian, the other from the Argentine—are seated in the row ahead of us on the bus:
Whore 1: "Have I gotten thinner . . . " She shoved a fleshy thigh into the aisle for all to see. "Or fatter?"
Whore 2: "Fatter."
Whore 1: "I'm not going to eat any more . . . (later) . . . What have you got in that bag?"
Whore 2: "Food."
Whore 1: "Good."
A few more miles down the road:
Whore 1: "See this Guatemalan crap I bought for my daughter? You know what she's going to say? . . . 'I don't want any crap from Guatemala. Why didn't you bring me something from the States?'"

They're fed up with Central America. They begin to compare little countries to little men, little men with little cocks.

"All that talk, and you can't even find it on the map. They want to tell you how great it is, but when they got their pants down, you got to grope for it in the dark. Nothing but complexes and violence and no money. And Chile—poof!—a revolution. What good is a revolution to us?"

*October 26, Managua*
*Gran Hotel $32.00*

The discovery of the birds. Sitting in a sidewalk restaurant at midnight, having dined on *tipitapa,* an excellent lake fish, and recovering from the long, hot, incredibly hot unairconditioned bus trip from Salvador, we noticed the white droppings on the pavement. We looked up and saw the birds. There they were—asleep wing-to-wing along the wires, occupying every nook and cranny of the dung-splashed façade of the municipal theatre—thousands of them. Row upon row, in close order like an army in repose (heads under wings) waiting out the night in the center of Managua. Definitely spooky, reminding me of Hitchcock's film. What are they waiting for? we wondered. We sensed an omen in this discovery.

An organic novel, a chemical novel, in which all elements—mystical, mental, and material—are shown to be interacting and influencing each other at all times. A novel in which the facts and assumptions of the past, the hopes and fears for the future, commingle and bear upon and impinge upon the realities of the present. As logical and predictable as elements combining to produce molecules.

Learn the local names for the Amazon, to use as a possible title.

Find out the names of the Spanish or Portuguese conquistadors who discovered it, who first descended or ascended the river.

An all-encompassing image of the great river ceaselessly flowing.

More scenes from along the road. At one stop we bought soft, white, ping-pong ball-sized turtle eggs, which the boys dig out of the sandy river bank. A local delicacy. The trick is to prick the shell with the point of a knife, squeeze, and the raw contents of the egg land in the back of your throat. One was enough for me. Oily aftertaste.

At one of the innumerable stops, a filthy market town, we jumped down from the bus to buy mangoes, cold Cokes, and the local newspaper. Un-iced fish displayed in the broiling sun. This sun too hot to stay for long in. Consequently, no sunburn. Dogs and pigs roam the muddy street. Madeleine, who once kept a pig as a pet, says that dogs and pigs will play together until the pig gets too rough. A pig will drive a dog away from food. Pigs are more intelligent.

A flock of chattering parrots jetted past. Good to see them again. A ferocious dog fight broke out in the market place. The initial indifference of the shoppers, their merriment when the blood began to flow, the raw violence of one dog killing another finally evoking applause.

*Local news item:*

Campesino wounded by an ice pick. *Tres mujeres de mal vivir* (whores)—Maria de Miseracordia, Ana Dolores, Yolanda Martinez Peña—have been taken into custody by the police.

On the ferry, the negro with the deep dark voice: he speaks Spanish slowly, perfectly, softly—with a kind of southern drawl. An American?

*More news:*

Swarm of Bees Kills 11 Animals

Recife, Brazil - (UPI) - A buzzing black cloud of African bees has swarmed over the farm of José Damiao da Silva, killing two horses, three mules, five goats, and a dog. Silva's wife, five children and four grandchildren were stung during the attack, and a farmhand was struck in the eye by a bullet Silva fired into the swarm.

Sweet revenge: The young American student, who had been riding with us all the way from Guatemala, found his seat taken by a large surly stranger who boarded at Managua. The bully refused to move, even threatened violence when the American showed him his designated seat ticket. Today, at the Panamanian frontier, the stranger was asked to open his suitcase, and the customs official lifted out a black, patent-leather lady's handbag. Inside the bag was a pair of pink panties. The officers howled with derisive laughter.

The young American, grinning in the background, sniggered, "Faggot. *Maricón!*"

My stomach is grumbling . . . must be that turtle egg . . . sounds like distant thunder.

*October 29, Panama. Hotel Continental $24*

The bloody remains of dozens of smashed mosquitoes on the wall do not bode well for a restful night. Our bed we've dubbed "The Grand Canyon." Big dip in the middle we inevitably roll into, no matter how hard we cling to the edge. No lock on the door. Went out and bought a latch and padlock. Screwed it on with my Swiss army knife. Then to the movies. Pasolini's *Decameron*. Those faces! Describe them! Get good at it.

From the movies to a cockfight:
The trained birds jump at each other, razor-sharp spurs aimed for the heart. Madeleine's animal-love doesn't cry out. There's no objection. She sheds no tears. She finds solace in animals, understands them better than people, but is not sentimental about them. She enjoys cockfights, bullfights less so. She admires these feathered gladiators in all their brutal luster.

Faces around the pit:
-the shadow of a mustache
-scruffy blond beard
-rotten teeth
-wrinkles like lava running down into the sea
-tiny blue eyes close together, freckles, a mass of curly black hair

Judge at the cockfight... toadface composed in Buddha-like

calm . . . counting money amidst the hysteria over the killing birds.

Panama: a tropical Harlem without . . . so far . . . the hostility.

From the cockfight to a jazz bar:
Face of the old black piano player, down from New Orleans. Smooth shiny face, without lines. He smiles a mysterious smile as he plays on and on, never having to look down at the keyboard which he strokes so effortlessly. The artist working every night for his living, dreamily oblivious of the frenzied gyrations of the dancers. Not unlike the old Gnaoua musicians who ply their trade on the Djmaa el Fna in Marrakesh.

From the jazz bar to the street:
The dusky hustler with the soft voice, whispering in my ear: "What you want, boss? Anything you want—I got it. Anything! See that big American car outside—air conditioned? It's mine. What you like?" When he gets the shove, the tone of his voice does not change. "That's all right, boss." Pats me on the back. "When you need something, you know where I am, right here. All the time. At your service."

*October 30. Hotel Lux $125.41*

Moved here from the other place after waging an all-night war against bugs. American mosquito dope totally ineffective against these Panamanian critters. A big room with plenty of closet space so we can unpack for a change. M habitually hangs up the clothes she has worn during the day, not in the closet but preferably near a window where they can air out overnight. Mother's rule.

## *4 PM*

In the Restaurant Panamar writing a letter to Paul Bowles in Tangier. The tropical rain coming down with a power and volume that mesmerizes. Cascading off roofs and gutters, turning streets into rivers and intersections into lakes where the automobiles plough through, hooting mournfully, bumping the fallen floating palm fronds. The parrots are silent. Oops, the lights just went out.

*Excerpt from my letter:*

Ah, the MAJIK of an American military base in the tropics. We visited the Canal Zone last night. The immaculate avenues, lined with royal palms, planted long ago, possibly with General McArthur or Ike, majors or colonels then, hands behind back, looking on. The tidy aspect of the wooden barracks, the churches (the Church of Christ characteristically lit by a blue neon sign you see along the roads through the rural American South), the U.S. Post Office, the gymnasium, the movie theatre, the Christian Science Reading Room, a branch of every New York bank, with old-fashioned façades masking modern offices. The police station: not a cop in sight—who needs them in such an orderly paradise? The various military installations, surrounded by well-tended lawns, the grass fairly luminous in the sultry night. A solitary marine stands guard in a pool of neon. The throb of the Canal. The hibiscus bushes, planted in rows—carefully trimmed. Hibiscus, if left untended, grows like crazy in the tropics. Beware, marine, the wild hibiscus! Oddly, the street lamps attract few insects, as if they, too, have been methodically eliminated. Not a candy wrapper to be seen. Peace, coziness and democracy pervade the sultry night. Yessir, Uncle Sam is looking after the world.

The Panamanian workers, on their way home in the gaily painted buses, laden with treasure from the PX, which they hardly take the trouble to conceal in huge brown paper bags. How many billions have been bilked, lost, casually mislaid or artfully purloined by the dark-skinned, cheerful, mustachioed Panamanians, who with such ease outwit the tough young marine, trained to kill with a single blow? And nailed to the door of every whorehouse and dive in the city, taped to the mirrors of the low-down cantina right across the street from the main entrance to the base: WE CASH U.S. GOVERNMENT CHECKS.

Not a Balboa (the fictitious local currency) to be seen anywhere in the country, nothing but dollars.

So far I've made little progress on the novel. Just notes and more notes. Scraps of paper that pile up like confetti in my briefcase. At each hotel where we think we'll stop for a few days I unpack the typewriter, clear a table, dig out the novel and set the alarm clock for an early hour. But resolve vanishes when I look out the window at the tropical scene and end up exploring the streets. This diary helps, but my nerves jangle when I'm not grappling with a major project. In two days we fly to Curaçao, thence to Surinam, where Madeleine has contacts. There we hope to rent a place where I can settle down and "hit the keys."

*October 31*

The special U.S. creep you run into in South America—bush pilot, civil engineer, agricultural expert, itinerant lumberjack, professional hunter, oil rigger, guide. He's been everywhere, seen everything, knows all the back roads, the inaccessible rivers. On first-name terms with bartenders in every Intercontinental and Hilton hotel from Mexico to Patagonia. Spanish-speaking, usually from California. Dark glasses, fair hair and pale blue eyes of the missionary. Something of both the missionary and the CIA about him. On a crusade of some sort, endlessly complaining about the backwardness of the natives whom he's down here to help out and screw up. Been everywhere with his big ideas and special equipment—airplanes, helicopters, oil rigs—and sneering cynicism.

*November 1*

The shoeshine boys of Panama. Whistling, quarrelling, making deals in their particular lingo incomprehensible to outsiders, they comprise a considerable force. Few have been initiated into the mysteries of their order, let alone introduced to the Chief himself. Their Telegraph and Information Patrol (T.I.P.) functions with remarkable efficiency, accuracy, and speed. Every word overheard from beneath the tables at cafés, bars, restaurants and barbershops, spoken by businessmen, bankers, politicians, military officers, smugglers, gunrunners, and criminals is recorded in the memories of the boys, transferred by word of mouth to the runners, who report to El Centro. No boy older than ten years. All illiterate and therefore memorize easily and automatically. Nothing is written down. Nobody suspects them. (T.I.P. operates under the assumption that officials and others with access to vital information like to have their shoes shined.) Dirty little angels, they may be collecting only nickels and dimes for their labors beneath the tables, but the intelligence they glean is worth thousands. They often converse in whistles. Even the youngest, no more than five or six years old, spit a great deal. Their whistling unaccountably makes the newspaper boys angry.

A letter from Dr. Kruesi, our family doctor, pointing out that the first signs of emphysema have appeared in the chest x-ray, part of the comprehensive physical examination I had before we set out on this trip. I am uncertain as to what this means, as I thought I had been cleared by a lung specialist in NY two or three years ago.

M's typically pitiless reaction to any sign of weakness: "Well, with your history of asthma, and your habit of lighting a cigarette before you can pick up a pen, what do you expect?"

This diary she calls my "book of words."

*November 3, Hotel Chu. Tobaga*

On this "isle of flowers" where M, Chula and I have come to spend the day, Francisco Pizarro built his ships before setting out for Peru. From here the first pineapple seed was sent to Hawaii. Huge grasshoppers *(langostinas)*. Graves of English pirates on the *morra.* Island peace, with the sound of waves splashing, the voices of children bathing, an old man in a hammock, snoring. No automobiles. The best anchorage in the Republic. Tomorrow we fly to another island—Curaçao.

Chula spends part of each day cleaning himself—according to M a clear sign of good health. Each green feather must be sought after among the others and preened and brushed—the long wing and tail feathers, and the downy breast feathers. The feathers behind the head are cleaned with the toe. The feet and nails must be manicured daily. An absolutely fearless little nipper.

*Newspaper item:*

"About mid-way on the trip, they entered an area of desolation hit by some mysterious jungle pestilence. Animal and bird life were non-existent. The only sounds were those made by horseflies, as big as a man's thumb, which buzzed around them constantly. Clouds of blood-sucking gnats hit them intermittently, leaving patches of red, itching blotches on their skin."

Today in Panama I bought a panama to replace my old straw that has worn out, at *Almacen Monteza, La Casa de los Sombreros,* whose logo, for some reason, is a wheel propelled by two bird wings. Size 7 1/8. Elegant thin black band. Now I'm ready for the Amazon.

Panamas don't come from Panama. They're woven in Ecuador from a palm-like plant called *paja toquilla.* They got their name from the transshipping 49ers (1849) who wore them against the sun while tramping across the Isthmus of Panama on their way to the California gold rush.

Palindrome: ¡A MAN, A PLAN, A CANAL PANAMA!

*November 5, Curaçao. Hotel San Marco $34.90*

Red flares across the harbor illuminate the enormous refinery. Red smoke and light are reflected upon the water like the fires of hell. Santa Petrolina I've dubbed it, symbol of the desecration of the environment, and it's going into the novel.

The Voodoo Gardens or Devil Gardens, known as HiFi, where the boys gather to sulk, play dominoes, and smoke the weed. Animal skulls hang from trees. Paintings of crocodiles and monsters with peace symbols for eyes, half-naked maidens with animal and human heads emerging from their underwear. "Don't kiss a boy who swears" . . . "peace" . . . "shaft" . . . "bridge over troubled water." The flaming serpent entwines the monsterman with one human foot and one rooster foot. The serpent has eaten his head; indeed the serpent's head (fanged jaws dripping blood) has replaced the monsterman's head on his shoulders; indeed, the monsterman already holds his own skull in his hand. Painted rubber tires. Peace, death and sex are the mottoes here. Same symbols all over the island—PEACE is DEATH and SEX is DEATH. SEX and DEATH bring PEACE . . .

Curaçao: The languor of the islands, lacking the Latin finger-popping zip. The blacks, tall, lope along with fluid movement. The girls, long-legged, round-assed, pointy breasts—fantastic figures. Coral beaches and iridescent fish. The poisonous manzanilla trees. Black-bellied she-goats eat paper bags and cigarette boxes. This is cactus and thorn tree country, with trapezoidal cottages. Many Jews here and the Chinese have found a lucrative refuge. The local people "lazy as hell." "A Portogee working for the Shell refinery (there are thousands of them over there, laboring beneath the flares) gets more done in one day than an islander in a week." So we are informed by a jewelry merchant in a bar. Good, let the Portogees do the lifting. The hard-working Portuguese, the sturdy Hollander—let them get the job done. The blacks, meanwhile, loll in their devil gardens and dream about sex and death and peace. Witchcraft is on the rise . . . it may be the next religion.

Madeleine seems happier here, more relaxed. Holland is her country, and Curaçao is Holland's island. She rattles away in her native tongue but understands only a few words of the local. Communications with Amsterdam are good. She called home and had a civil conversation with her mother. Her Uncle Daan still in Tangier, coping with cancer. No crisis . . . yet.

On the way to Boca Tabla, where the waves shake the caves, we asked directions from a black man sitting on a fence. Naked to the waist, right shoulder and breast a livid white, the rest of him speckled with bright pink spots. An advanced case of vitiligo. I have it myself, but nothing like this poor guy. He sat there, fascinated, absorbed, picking at it—picking off his black skin. Dumb, dead eyes registering nothing, mumbling mumbo jumbo, picking at the pink and white spots. We passed by again, half expecting him (he who had given us directions to the beach in a language neither of us could understand) to be all pink and white to the waist, half black man half albino . . . but he'd gone.

*papiamente* = talking; *toko* (Malay) = shop

The firstborn make poor mates she says. (She has three younger brothers.)

The Queen Emma Floating (pontoon) Bridge. A private concession charges 2 cents ˇˇ for people wearing shoes. The bare-footed pass for free.

*November 7, Paramaribo, Surinam. Hotel Kersten $138.00*

On the dashboard of our taxi from the airport:

WALDO IS YOUR DRIVER NOT YOU

Not many cities like this left in the world, I should imagine. Built entirely of wood, many of the tall buildings, multi-balconied, date back to the 17th and 18th centuries. The cathedral also of wood, so is the mosque. Massive mahogany trees shade the streets. Not unnaturally the citizens fear fire. A handful of revolutionaries could easily set the place alight. It has happened before. The local population, a legacy of the Dutch colonial empire, is a mixture of Asian, African, European, and American Indian races. Very few white faces about. Temperature normal (98.6°), humidity 100% and, just like Holland, no shoeshine boys.

Madeleine goes barefoot, even in the city. She kicks off her shoes every chance she gets. I tell her she's going to step on a nail and get an infection, but "she loves to feel the wiggle of her toes."

The morning of our very first day we went to the Staaten van Surinam or parliament, to hear a debate (in Dutch) about motors in steamboats, and met, through Madeleine's Dutch contacts, Mr Jules Sednÿ, the prime minister. An affable, rotund black man, tonight he is taking us to the U.S. Consulate to listen to the American election returns. Saturday he has invited us to go with him by private plane to his fishing camp in the jungle.

The following is a rough outline of the local political roster in the Staaten, as related to us by the bartender in our hotel:

| The ruling coalition: | |
|---|---|
| P.N.P.-Progressive National Party (Creole) | 8 seats |
| V.H.P.-United Hindustani Party (Hindu) | 15 seats |
| P.S.V.-Progressive Surinam Folkparty (Creole) | 2 seats |
| | 25 seats |
| **The opposition:** | |
| N.P.S.-National Party of Surinam* (Creole) | 11 seats |
| K.I.P.-Indonesian Party | 1 seat |
| B.P.S.-Bushnegro Party | 1 seat |
| S.D.S.-Surinam Democratic Party | 0 seats |
| P.N.R.-National Republican Party (Creole) | 1 seat |
| (and one other he couldn't think of) | 2 seats |
| | 16 seats |

The P.N.P., P.S.V., and P.N.R. all used to be part of the main N.P.S., but splintered off following disputes.

Politics: the Hindus are the largest, best financed and best organized party but contrive not to win for fear of being massacred by the blacks. Here, as in Africa, the Hindus' focused mercantile purpose and relentless commercial success are envied and resented.

M suffers from poor circulation in the legs. After that walk her ankles were swollen. Lying on her back in bed, she propped her feet against the wall while I, rubbing downward, massaged her ankles and calves. The swelling disappeared quickly.

*November 8*

A sudden rainstorm during breakfast. The breeze ruffled the

* The bartender's party.

tablecloths in the open-air dining room as the waitress hurried to fasten the shutters. Dutch breakfast: cheese and pressed tongue. One is supposed to butter the bread, as one does in Holland, cover with a broad slice of cheese and slab of tongue, and eat with a knife and fork. The rain abated, but the waitress opened the shutters prematurely, allowing the wind to disturb the tablecloths once more to the irritation of the blonde Dutch proprietress, who had just smoothed them out. From outside the window, barbaric screeching noises are heard. Otherwise, the town, it being a holiday, is quiet.

Firecrackers. A new moon. The Moslems are celebrating the end of Ramadan. Their mosque is an impressive painted wooden building, ornate but stately, with 5 minaret-like towers and an onion-shaped cupola. Back in our beloved Marrakesh the faithful will be returning to normal after the month of fasting.

The 82-year-old black grandmother, who sells green bananas on the front steps of the hotel, declares she's lived in Holland and Indonesia, but knew that one day she had to return to Surinam.

"So here I am, children. You don't begrudge a grandmother five cents change, do you?"

The nickels here are square.

Grandmother rolls a cigarette. Very thin cigarettes are rolled here. The paper is carefully creased and torn down the middle; one half is discarded before the cigarette is rolled. The result resembles a stingy joint.

Moseying along the quayside, I dreamily sized up the Brazilian trading schooners in port. Can we find one to take us to Bel^én at the mouth of the Amazon? One also takes, I am told, one's life in one's hands. Romantic as they look, these ships are manned by lawless contrabanders who think nothing of slitting your throat, emptying your pockets, and feeding you to the sharks . . .

The P.M.'s joke. One party promises security "from cradle to grave"; the next "from womb to tomb"; and the next "from erection to resurrection."

Jealousy: repetitions of the hated image ripping the brain apart. Each image with slight but significant variation is voluptuously and hideously repeated through the sleepless night, a horror film of one's own making which one is forced to attend, nailed to the seat.

Such is the power of the novel, reading *Under the Volcano* makes me envy the freedom, the recklessness, the vision of the drunkard.

As if we didn't already have enough luggage to haul around, I am having a suit made, a beautiful white linen suit, by R. Hanief & Son, Indian tailors. Fifty bucks for the suit plus two shirts.

Among the multitude aboard the ferry *To Meerzorg* (More Care or More Sorrow):
The process of purchasing a ferryboat ticket becomes a hassle, as the lithe dark-skinned native boys slither along the wall to squeeze past me in line, brazenly attempt to pick my pocket and, while I scold them, manage to steal my handkerchief. The Indians, Creoles, Chinese, and Indonesians squabble in incomprehensible polyglot with the ticket-seller over—what? Black man with large crooked teeth, like bleached tombstones canting this way and that in an ancient cemetery. An albino negro, with ugly little coils of black hair springing from milky skin. Chinese negroes, Indonesian negroes, slant-eyed Hindus, freckle-faced Chinese—every mixed-blood freak is to be found here in Surinam. The Hindu with thick black hair,

heavily oiled and brushed straight back, beads of sweat standing out just below the hairline. Long feathery eyelashes give him a gentle mien, heaviness of neck and jowl notwithstanding. Pretty Indonesian girls with broad flaring nostrils, pig-like extremity to their nearly bridgeless noses, voluptuous full lips, fine skin. (Black skin appears much coarser.) A fair-skinned Creole woman. Within the immaculate patterned hairstyles of the young negro girls, a multitude of braids like the tails of tiny animals hiding in the wool.

Steatopygia much in evidence here . . . also the gruesome elephantiasis.

Children with the somber faces of adults. Old folks with the silly expressions of children. The fragility in those Indonesian faces. Voluptuous black girl, breasts bulging beneath her thin cotton print dress, pouting pink lower lip—patina of perspiration makes black skin glisten. How can skin seem so smooth? A firecracker exploded. Black people laughed when I jumped. The glittering eyes of the young Indonesian. The Indian with the long greasy hair and crazy eye. Children clinging like monkeys. Very few children.

All these people of various races, religions and colors, whose ancestors were brought by their Dutch masters from the four corners of the empire to dig canals and drain the sweltering swamps of South America—the local Indians wouldn't do it—mingle in this tropical seaport. As co-inhabitants of a limited space they seem to bear a pragmatic tolerance for one another, but not love. All love goes toward the children and the family—i.e., survival. Gentle, weak, poor, and humble as they may appear, you get the feeling they would be at each other's throats at the drop of a hat. The Teutons aren't the only people nurturing final solution plans for other races.

Tropic complaint—this heat! Repudiating all energy and enterprise, discouraging initiative and imagination, stunting growth (except for the sexual parts), causing slowdowns, breakdowns, mismanagement, and incompetence.IBM directed from a hammock in a grass shack. Scientific accomplishment beneath a swinging ceiling fan, dispelling 100° heat, 100% humidity, flies, anopheles mosquitoes, and the stink of rotting fruit. Encouraging sloth, alcoholism, laziness, greed, graft, and fornication. Enlarging sexual parts—seam-splitting young breasts and bulging cocks that point south, east, west, mainly north. Snakes, tarantulas, scorpions, centipedes, and cockroaches hold their ground. Brilliance contained in a bottle of rum.

*November 9*

I have paid $600 to one Jytta Elgaard, Danish girl guide, for a 7-8 day canoe trip up the Marowijne River to visit the Bushnegro and Indian tribes who live in the headwaters.

*November 10*

Madeleine's birthday tomorrow. Thirty-one years old. She's a good travelling companion, speaks several languages, and never complains. 5' 9" tall, physically strong, she doesn't mind roughing it. She enjoys a physical challenge. She had to compete with three brothers. As the eldest, she had to stick up for them in school. She mends my clothes, sews on buttons with needle and thread from her sewing kit, and cuts my hair once a week. Her erect posture is the result of her Scots nanny jamming a wire coat hanger down the back of her blouse each time she slumped at the breakfast table.

Our hotel room overlooks the red tin roofs of this tropical

seaport, nestled beneath the massive mahogany trees which provide shade for the streets of Paramaribo.

*November 11*

Today, as a birthday present for Madeleine, the P.M. is taking us by private plane to his jungle hideaway for two days' fishing.

Name of Surinam's airport: HOPE AND SORROW

Kayserburg. From the air, a jungle road appears as a smooth red ditch dug through the green carpet of trees. The carpet becomes more variegated as the plane descends—dangerously, through banks of dense cloud—and one makes out mauve trees, yellow flowering trees, and many dead ones held upright within the forest's grip, unable to fall. A gleam of reflected sunlight follows us across the waterways of the swamp.

Florescent blue butterflies float through the leafy green cathedral of the rain forest like wandering souls from another distant age.

The *kappassie* or capybara (in Peru he's called *ronsocco*) the world's largest rodent, which I have not yet seen, lives in sinister symbiosis with the deadly bushmaster, which I have not seen yet either, and hope never to see. It reputedly has the longest fangs of any poisonous serpent, and its venom softens and dissolves the flesh, so it can eat more. The *kappassie* digs the hole; the bushmaster moves in and guards it.

The howler monkeys: unseen, moving through the forest, now near, now far, a whole family of them. Their voices in the distance made me think of vague whisperings from beyond the grave. They became louder as the troupe drew near, moaning and crying, as they spoke of forest spirits and mimicked the rumbling pleas of the shades of extinct animals entombed in mighty trees. At 4.30 in the morning they reached the far edge of the landing strip, where their shouts woke us up with our hair standing on end.

These negro women who wait on us possess tremendous vitality and physical strength. Nothing indefinite about them.

Characters (for a future novel):
The solitary Dutchman, empire relinquished, toils in this outpost on the edge of civilization. The Indian transplanted from his native land. The Chinaman, the Bushnegro—each a caricature and embodiment of his race.

Tapoena Doro: Surinamese for tap on the door. Harp vines tremble in a shaft of sunlight (you have to imagine the music). Fish scales and vulture feathers, the cry of the fish hawk, and the wall of her indifference.

Fishing. I didn't know quite what we were going for—tarpon, I'd hoped, or some other tropical fighting fish, but none of that. Not a fishing rod in camp. The P.M. and his assorted henchmen and hangers-on sit in deck chairs along the muddy bank and throw handlines into the chocolate water. In the mid-day heat the entire government of Surinam has fallen asleep, handlines attached to their big toes. Every now and then one will haul out a sluggish catfish which nobody eats.
*Cat on a Hot Tin Roof*: delayed commentary on the film we saw in Panama. Entertaining, full of his genius, sympathy, and humanity, but essentially lightweight, even in the terms to which it aspires, and already dated beyond Aeschylus.

The dignity of the profession (writing): the peace and excitement this journal has given me. The freedom, the wildness of thought entertained and preserved, with the essential non-interference feeding the pleasure of creation.

My head is sore from banging it against the wall. My jealousy and her indifference—what a combo.

As we sipped whiskey by the campfire, the P.M. leafed through a copy of *The Attempt* which I had just signed for him and engagingly inquired about my writing. I explained the purpose of the trip and my failure, so far, to find a place to settle down for a while and focus on the new book. He owns a shackette on the outskirts of Parbo (where, I am told, he takes his girls), near the river, which he offered to lend us for as long as we want, where I can set up shop and get on with the novel. The subtext, of course, is Madeleine. What with her aristocratic Dutch background and fashionable European clothes, she has become the star attraction and something of a celebrity in provincial Paramaribo. The P.M. wants her to stick around for as long as possible.

S.S.P.I. for the huge quantities of phlegm I keep bringing up. Sat. Sol. Potassium Iodide drops in water.

*November 13*

On the Marowijne or Maroni River, which divides Surinam from French Guiana. First day out from Albina, with a quick stop in St. Laurent on the French side to pick up Dietmar, a German "philanthropic anthropologist," and—what I learned in Peru and Guatemala to be a vital accessory for hot and sweaty jungle river trips—several bottles of booze, in this case Caribbean rum dark as the girl on the label. La Negrita.

With us on board the dugout canoe Ardjuna (Viano's

Tours) are Jytta—our Danish girl guide, Viano—chief boatman (and, Madeleine whispers, Jytta's lover), Aleké—assistant boatman, and our bowboy, Yamaa.

Yamaa in hispanicized Moroccan Arabic means mosque and also Friday—the day on which devout Moslems go to the mosque. Therefore Yamaa is our boy Friday. He does all the odd jobs, like washing dishes, but mainly he bails out the canoe. At ten years he is already an expert riverboy and could probably navigate this river on his own, if necessary. For him, as for us, we are embarking on a grand adventure. On his head he wears a plastic orange mesh onion sack which makes him look like a black child-knight out of the Middle Ages, if such a person ever existed. He stands in the bow holding a long pole, gauging the depth and keeping an eye out for rocks.

Yamaa has a friend whom I've dubbed "the fish-boy of Albina." He never comes out of the water. He stays in the river all day, swimming among the canoes and other craft half drawn up on the mud. In the evening, Yamaa says, his mother comes down to throw food from the shore, like you would feed a fish.

First night: we stopped in Akatia, one of the Bushnegro settlements not yet Christianized by the missionaries. We entered the village through a grass-fringed gateway erected to brush off evil river spirits.

Viano, our leader, of Herculean physique, is a great raconteur and gossip. Wearing a pair of skimpy shorts, he sits by the campfire in the swept mud clearing, speaking TakiTaki—a mixture, as far as I can make out, of English, Dutch, Spanish, Portuguese and one of the bird languages of Africa. To me it sounds like baby talk or a tape running at high speed. He's entertaining a bevy of almost completely naked black ladies, some young, some old, telling them "how it really is." The women whoop with laughter and slap their knees. Isolated in the forest, their only news comes via the river, and they hang on every word uttered by this muscle-bound trouba-

The Maroni River is well populated, with one tiny Bushnegro village after another visible along the bank. A notable absence of game. Oops—the first alligator . . . a big one. A sinister swirl of mud by the bank. Dietmar spotted it.

These Bushnegroes, descendants of runaway slaves, feel and express strong attachment for their ancestral home in Africa. Some, I am told, still speak Kromati, which their paramount chiefs used when they visited Ghana. The most successful means of communication with their African brothers, however, was via the drum. The same music still lives on, in the rain forests on both sides of the Atlantic.

The ceiba or *kankan tribong* tree is considered holy and therefore is not used for making dugout canoes. (The Ardjuna was hollowed from the trunk of another species of huge tree, with side boards added.) The ceibas with their massive flying buttress-like roots, as though God rolled up his sleeves and built this one Himself, dominate the greasy yellow bank. The enticing yellow sand beaches we must avoid. So far, the river has been broad and calm, interrupted by an occasional light rapid, as we make a smooth and effortless passage. Unfortunately, the thunder and vibrations from the motor blot out all other sound. With night, silence descends over the jungle like an opaque curtain. We sleep soundly in our hammocks with the whisper of the river in our ears.

"There is no more luxurious bed than a hammock, yielding and resistant, as though you were cradled in air . . . "

—H. M. Tomlinson, *The Sea and The Jungle*

The trick for sleeping comfortably is to stretch out diagonally. This position flattens the hammock and you wake in the morning without a crick in your back.

Madeleine and I sling ours side by side so we can reach out and reassuringly hold hands when the howler monkeys fill the jungle with their banshee roars or when other unknown sounds from close by startle one or both of us awake. Viano says a *tigre* or jaguar made the sharp coughing noise we heard last night.

The rainy season having only just begun, the river is still shallow this time of year, and Viano takes over the important bow position. We are passing through the Nassau Mountains, and tremendous groves of bamboo clot the banks. The slash and burn technique is employed to clear the land for cultivation of the all-important manioc. A new field yields a good crop for five or six years only and is then left fallow for the jungle to reclaim.

The bites of jungle lice raise itchy red welts. To keep them from spreading, we rub on kerosene.

With the rapids becoming more difficult, more frequent, and more dangerous, we begin to appreciate the skill and experience of the boatmen. We mount one hill of brown water after another. We could easily become lost among the maze of islands. The channel, a half-mile across an hour ago, has narrowed to ten feet. Even when the river widens again, it deceives. Water, hundreds of yards across, may be only a foot deep, with little current to mark the hazards.

We have seen a piranha—impaled on a stick, drying in the sun, prior to being smoked, prior to being eaten . . .

A chance encounter with Viano's sister (also Yamaa's mother), who has a camp on an island across the river from her cassava (manioc) field. Viano cut the motor and we drifted on the tree-draped lagoon, as the woman poled towards us. The women's canoes are easily distinguishable from the men's, as patterns of nails decorate the prow and stern and the sides are gaily painted. The canoes are presents from their husbands.

The voices of mother and son carried across the water in an exchange that sounded like verse. Voices travel easily over water, and the ears of these people are keen. A man speaking in a normal tone of voice is heard and answered from two hundred yards. The chatter was about Viano's niece, who had been given a good beating by Viano's brother for leaving her husband, even though she received barely enough money from him to support herself and her five children.

The woman had a wiry muscular frame similar to that of a man, tired flapping breasts notwithstanding. We gave her bread and rolls and one cigarette. A woman, I am told, will smoke one cigarette before going to bed. She gave us tapioca root, manioc, and bananas. Gifts are continually being exchanged here.

(Earlier, we had visited Aleké's village, where we were presented with sugar cane and tapir meat. His little son burst into tears when we went off.)

Afterwards, we churned through a series of narrow, twisting rapids—the most challenging yet. Aleké, the shy one, doffed his clothes. Clad in a bathing suit and displaying a muscular back a sculptor would drool over, he manned the bow. Water splashed in as the canoe mounted one brown hill after another. We bailed frantically with calabashes. At the Stoelmaneisland Rapids we were advised to get out and walk, carrying "anything we don't want to lose," which turned out to be just about everything. But Viano & Co. brought the ship through.

*Names of rapids:*

The first—*Man Barie* = Man Scream—there being many

electric eels about.
The second—*Siengatete* = Weaving Thread.
The third—*Poloegoedoe* = Trouble Maker, or Spoiler of Goods, or Spoiling Richness, or Taking Out The Most Valuable Goods (from the canoe before attempting passage.)

At Stoelmanseisland we stopped for some cold beer before setting off on the Lawa River.

A dead vulture on a crucifix: an offering to the river god. The vulture flies the highest and therefore is considered to be the wisest bird.

*November 15*

Second night spent at Grand Santi in French Guiana, a large village complete with a native shop. Madeleine discovered her favourite Gauloise cigarettes, and we stocked up on toilet paper. Civilization: electricity, outhouses, and two French *responsables* who looked over our passports.

M, her hammock close to mine, ground her teeth all night, which surprised me, as she seemed relaxed and happy on this particular trip far from home. Or have I got it wrong again? It may appear we are travelling light, one basket of clothes each and dressed in shorts or bathing suits most of the time, but even in this wilderness I cannot afford to ignore the heavy emotional baggage we never left behind.

The technique for passing over a shoal or submerged rock which cannot be avoided is for the motorman to give one final burst of power before lifting the propeller clear of the water, as the bowman with his pole supplies an extra increment of momentum. The canoe slides up and over, often with a bump. As if he himself has been hurt, Viano groans loudly each time the propeller grinds against a rock. In some places, the waterway ahead appears to be completely closed by rock or fallen trees, but we always manage to thread our way through.

According to Jytta, the Indians are extremely credulous and therefore vulnerable. You can do anything with them. The Bushnegroes, on the other hand, are more resilient, more used to the ways of the white man, and therefore less susceptible to his influence. Nevertheless these riverine civilizations are all doomed, she says—their days numbered by so-called progress.

The range of these people's experience may not be wide, but within their watery domain they are deeply knowledgeable, proficient at everything they do, but vulnerable to encroaching "civilization," and that includes us.

Yamaa, insisting that I take a photo of "him alone," posed with his arms crossed imperiously across his chest, chin thrust upwards, like some miniature African potentate. This one might be the new Bonnie . . .

A pair of toucans flit like phantoms through the trees. The *banabecky* (banana beak) is a yellow-billed weaver. Last night I dreamed about snakes, catching them just behind the head with the bare hand.

Indian saying: "The waterfall is singing, I will find my song when I find my freedom."

After detouring all morning among serpentine, rocky passages, some of which were no wider than the gondola, and where, at times, we all had to get out and, standing waist deep in the surging torrent, help push our craft up a virtual wall of water, we arrived at the top of Links-i-Deed (at the left side, death) Rapids.

Worn out from our efforts we stopped, rested, and had a look. A profusion of boulders, some of which were the size of small houses, bled white water like milky epaulettes. The main current snaked through at race-horse speed. These rapids are said to conceal "rolling boulders," unstable and threatening for canoes. One boulder in particular moves or is so shaky that people believe that something underneath pushes it. An evil spirit. The soul of a drowned riverman yearning for company. It is also said that the stern of a boat, where the motor is attached, acts as a kind of lodestone, drawing trouble behind it. And there on the left side of the rapids (the death side), high and dry on the rocks, lay a canoe just like ours, splintered and battered, its back broken in the middle. And, like the smell of death, the vegetal stink of the forest . . .

The Lawa River: more intimate than the broader Maroni. When we are not struggling over rapids and waterfalls, we glide peacefully across placid lagoons where the trees bend tunnel-like over our heads, with lianas trailing lightly in the water. The virginal solitude conveys a mystery, as if we are the first to pass this way. We have seen and heard numerous Chulas and a strange little bat-like, gray-brown bird that lands on top but clings to the bottom side of a branch.

How shall I describe the dense mass of foliage that is the jungle? The erect, white-hulled ceibas, like so many Greek columns, support a maze of vines, some of which are caught in a tangle, while others hang straight down like unattended trapeze ropes or pale harp strings, daintily stroking the water to emit some unheard music. Flowers and the wild white waterbirds . . . clusters of phoebus butterflies dance in shafts of sunlight like petals or confetti thrown in the wind. They live, I am told, but for 24 hours.

Light, falling through the sieve of leaves and branches, sprinkles the water. All about us lurk the phantom forms of animals and birds, which more often than not turn out to be stones or logs or stumps or a piece of driftwood, or a yellow leaf catching a beam of light. Brilliantly colored toucans croak in the trees where they pick at the fruit. A great white heron stretches one wing and watches from a branch as we toil up yet another watery slope, go forth upon yet another watery plain.

Our rivermen have made this trip hundreds of times, the river is all they know, yet each passage requires the sum of all their skill and strength and careful deliberation. As we approach one treacherous *malpaso* after another, Aleké's muscular frame is taut with strain. With his pole he fends off boulders, and Viano is exhausted at the end of each day. But who does not envy the special skill and knowledge of the riverman, or give thanks for it? On the river, he alone is the guarantee of safety, but the river, being king, must never be challenged. If man respects the river, from time to time he will receive a reward.

Following the successful passage of another dangerous rapid, Viano chants the African song of relaxation and celebration; sometimes, at the most hazardous moment, a shot of rum may be required for a little Dutch courage.

On the river, nothing is taken for granted. The river disposes, dealing both life and death as it pleases.

Few people to be seen here, but white flags mark their shrines in little clearings along the bank. In the afternoon we passed Benzdorp, once the gold-mining center on the river. Some gold is still brought out. This is where Jytta's black "Mama," whom we met in Albina, came in 1915 looking for her lost brother, whom she finally found after laboring for two years in the goldfields. The river has been wide, calm, and lake-like for many miles now, with numerous noble ceibas raising their symmetrical umbrella-like crowns above the treeline along the shore.

Certain creatures, such as the bushmaster, which may bring bad luck or are dangerous, should not be mentioned, lest they be summoned by the sound of their names. Dietmar nevertheless foolishly persists in blabbing in an authoritative (so he thinks) but joking manner about all the lurking dangers. This irritates Madeleine and Jytta, both of whom speak and understand German, both of whom were born in Nazi-occupied countries. Jytta said this talk would make Viano angry if he knew what Dietmar was saying. This indiscreet fellow is beginning to get on everyone's nerves.

Sturdy Bushnegro women stand in a cockeyed manner, big ass stuck out, with shoulders forward and a black hand on the sleek black bottom. Murmuring and cooing like birds, these people greet one another with a gentleness and consideration. When conversing, they do not look at each other—it is considered impolite to do so.

In the branches of a tree above this hut where we have stopped to spend the third night, a flock of *banabeckies*, or weavers, continuously chatter from their pouch-like nests. A kind of mynah bird, variously colored—all black, or black and yellow, or black and red.

*November 16*

The *banabeckies'* cries wake us at dawn.

"Wake up! Wake up! What for? What for? Chopchop! Chopchop!"

They can even imitate whirring motorboat noises. Yamaa is sulking because they crapped on the breakfast dishes he left by the river, so he had to wash them again.

Viano warns us again not to wade off the beaches. A stingray barb can cause three months of excruciating pain . . .

We have seen the first Indian. All of a sudden, he materialized. There he was—standing in a canoe, bow and fishing arrow in hand, a handsome fellow with long wavy hair . . . lithe body lighter and leaner than those of the muscle-bound Bushnegroes.

We have arrived at Maripasoula, which marks the end of Djuka and the beginning of Indian territory. Cows wander about, as do Indians in red loin cloths *(camisas)*. We purchased grape juice, red wine, and downed cold Heinekens while listening to a French radio broadcast, transmitted from Paris. The tricolor—in how many far-flung outposts has that flag been flown? One of the most exotic was Beni-Abbès, Algeria . . . ragged pennant fluttering from the Foreign Legion fort on the edge of the great sand desert. At Paul Bowles' suggestion, Joe and I had driven there from Tangier back in 1964. Every place in North Africa where he told us to go, we went, and were never disappointed.

When Dietmar raises his voice in anger or pique, it loses the American accent he has been trying to cultivate and becomes distinctly thicker, more Germanic.

"You dink I don't know dat? Vy, dis iz my zixd trip indo de chungle!"

Today, reflecting upon yesterday's perilous toils through the rapids, I think of the many scary moments when our canoe and all its cargo could have been lost, had the boatmen made one false move or bad decision. Viano's air of reckless vitality belies a consummate skill and constant vigilance. And he does this every day.

Jytta hides the booze. If the Indians see it, they'll pester us for it, and they get drunk and angry right away. She and Viano are business partners and lovers. They work well as a team, dividing the chores between them.

Aleké, naked to the waist, looks almost scholarly in Madeleine's dark glasses, which she has lent him to protect his eyes from the wind.

When Viano and Aleké argue about a collision with a submerged rock, about whose fault it was, both voices retain tones of reason and restraint. In the end, lack of communication is blamed. Aleké is a thinking bowman, not irresponsible like others, a fact which Viano must get accustomed to. As a gesture of reconciliation, Viano passes his bowl of cassava, from his position in the stern, to Aleké in the bow. This pleases Jytta.

Both routinely fish with bow and arrow whenever we stop, although nothing yet has been caught. Now Madeleine has found a lovely long fishing arrow floating in the water and retrieved it. Fashioned from a strong but hollow reed to make them light, fishing arrows measure about six feet in length. They are painted and feathered with pinions from a parrot's wing, and tipped with a barbed wooden point two feet long, carved from some incredibly hard wood that looks like palm but is not. The feathers are attached in spiral, so the shaft rotates in flight, giving it truer aim, like a bullet fired from a rifle.

Adult men and women will not touch leftover food, so yesterday's rice, reheated, is eaten by Yamaa.

The large, bright-green flat-topped tree is known as *quatacama* or Monkey-bed tree. (Spider monkey.)

We stopped in an Indian village to pick up an Indian guide for the remainder of the trip upstream. He now shares the bow position with Aleké. A handsome chap, his pretty young wife has just waved goodbye. So different these people are from the Africans, more lightly muscled, with bird-like delicate but strong physiques. A warm red color, which the women embellish with red dye *(rukuh)*. Their villages are more spacious than those of the Bushnegroes. An old squaw was tickled by the fact that we come from so many different countries. All Indians wear the red loincloth. The women's asses are left bare, while the men's are covered. Our guide came aboard carrying a small plastic imitation leather suitcase and has quickly changed from loincloth to bathing suit. More round-shouldered than Aleké who is built like a prizefighter, his muscles appear more supple, less bunchy. (More fat beneath the skin, Jytta points out.) The sleek Indian body fairly glows from within.

*November 17*

I thought I had an idea for a new work routine, but have already had to abandon it. Aside from this diary, I am getting little writing done on this trip even though fresh ideas for the novel are churning inside my head. We are on the boat most of the day, evenings are spent setting up camp, and in the tropics darkness comes on with a rush.

This morning I slipped out of my hammock at dawn. In the silence of the forest (the first light of day having stilled the all-night roar of the insects), mist clotted among the trees; a few half-hearted hoots signalled that the birds were just beginning to wake up.

Placing my typewriter on a low, pre-selected stump, I sat down before it, cross-legged in the dirt, inserted a sheet of paper and was just about to hit the keys when a mass of ants—the red, stinging variety—poured out of the wood like a tide of molasses.

Snatching away the typewriter before it was overrun, I proceeded to another stump, giving it a couple of kicks to make sure that no aggressive insects dwelled within. I had typed less than half a page when something made me look up. A crowd of naked people was standing behind me. Women, children, a few old men. The alien clacking sound made by my typewriter had woken up the entire village.

In the village of Antecume Pata *(Village pilot pour la defense des Wayana).*

Madeleine and I have passed a sunny afternoon playing waterfall games and shooting rapids with the seductively naked Indian children, all of whom speak some French. They have taught me how to hide from my enemies in the water. The trick is to crouch or lie below a boulder over which water is flowing and where, invisible to the pursuing tribe, you are able to breathe in the bubble of air behind the waterfall.

This spacious village, agreeably located on a bank high above the river, is breezy and cool, and the rush of the river soothes the ears. Tame macaws wander about, dragging their long tails. Dusk nears, the last of the sunlight filters through the tall trees, and silent lightning laces a distant thunderhead. We have slung our hammocks in a large open central hut. An unruly macaw had to be forcibly evicted before we could move in. Now he complains in a hoarse screeching dialogue with another parrot on the other side of the village.

The Chief—good-looking, virile and strong despite having one leg shorter than the other—displays beautiful bows and arrows which he wishes to sell us. Now comes the sound of an Indian flute.

Indians returning from a hunting expedition share a dish of cassava. These hot young men, at the peak of their strength, are only seventeen or eighteen years old. Strong, silent, beautifully built, their skins fairly glowing red, they move with supple, animal-like fluidity. Except for the scalp, they pluck out every hair from their bodies, even the eyelashes. A pair of tweezers is a prized possession. Apparently the test of virility is to bring on a hive of wasps . . .

Everyone, including the Chief, begs for everything we have. We have to be careful with the booze, hiding it and re-hiding it, as the Indians shamelessly paw through our gear.

Apparently there's going to be a fiesta of some sort tomorrow night . . .

Little Indian boy . . . please stop . . . no, go on—tickling my feet! Seduction is their game. They swim like minnows and want to hold hands all the time. (Today—I don't know why I know this—happens to be the Emperor Tiberius's birthday.) Indian children approach on tiptoe and whisper in my ear, so close their breath tickles:

*"Bonbon!"*

And Madeleine sees these little Indian children being hugged by their mamas. She smiles, but when she turns away from this show of maternal affection, her eyes glisten with tears.

Yamaa regards the Indians with typical African haughtiness. To prove his superiority, he has a tin horn which he blows repeatedly. The sound uncannily evokes the distant late-night whistle of the DL&W—the Delaware, Lakawanna and Western (a.k.a. the Delay, Linger & Wait) commuter train between Hoboken and Morristown, NJ—that used to spook my American childhood summer nights.

A boy, twelve or thirteen, already husky and strong, is a half-caste. We are told that his father was German, which Dietmar takes as a personal insult. His mother a local Indian girl. The boy's hair is a dirty blond. European blood has coarsened the pure Indian features; his skin is also rougher than that of his half-brothers. The cheek beneath one eye has been repeatedly burned with hot irons, causing the eye to run permanently. His face is pathetically twisted from these tortures. Otherwise, he appears to be a complete member of the tribe, but one who must serve as a scapegoat when troubles arise and blame must be apportioned. Like the other children, he speaks a little French, and evidently feels some kinship with white strangers. Tomorrow, he will take us walking in the jungle.

Darkness has fallen . . . ping of mosquitoes in the air. The extraordinarily neat and efficient campfires both Indians and Bushnegroes make, with logs like the spokes of a wheel meeting in the center. Every now and then someone sticks out a toe to nudge the spokes forward, and the flame burns on.

As we were going down to the river for an after-dinner swim, the Chief, apparently thinking we were on our way to relieve ourselves, followed and very politely instructed us where to make kaka. Not on the riverbank, as so many French, German, and American visitors have done; not on the rocks, which goes against the village rule; but in the water, preferably rushing water, in the rapids below the wash area. Patting his butt with one hand, he points with the other to appropriate place.

*November 18*

In the jungle, nothing grows alone, nothing grows free. Each tree, bush, vine or flower supports or is supported by another; springs from or is smothered by another; leans against or is leaned against; hangs from or is hung from. Each bears a burden of encumbering moss or fungus, the devouring mushroom, the parasitic orchid and the imprint of lichens. All sprout from death. The garden is death, the soil is death, the fertilizer is death. Death gives life, is the origin of all growth; all life in the jungle is rooted in death.

The great flat-topped monkey-bed tree, falling, cuts a swath of light, creating a glade where new life instantly germinates, quickly swallowing all light and space. The young sapling, vine-strangled, enfolds the lethal parasite within layers of its own bark—the embrace of death. The thicker, stronger vine, unable to stand alone, draws life from the young tree and must, when the stunted, prematurely withered host finally succumbs, perish with it. The history of the forest is recorded in its many-layered floor, reeking with vegetal stink of new life stubbornly emerging. The ruthless struggle of the vegetable world.

*3 PM: hammock time . . .*

*Maati* = friend. Derived from the word "mate"?

The sight of these naked Indian women quickly dispels any aesthetic or sexual notions about breasts. They are about as attractive as dugs on a bitch. As a man, one is grateful not to have those flapping appendages.

Native reasoning (Viano): "If I find a man with my wife, I give him a good beating, if he's smaller than I am. If he's bigger, I give her a good beating."

This morning, on our walk through the jungle, our half-caste guide pointed out a woodpecker, a hummingbird, a lime-green snake; but most beautiful of all was the lacy mushroom.

Our "philanthropic anthropologist" has turned out to be a

trader.

The Indians say "Don't stay alone by the river at night, or the water sprites will come for you." (This last written by moonlight, Nov. 18 '72.)

*November 19*

In the jungle, our day begins at daybreak, and it ends at nightfall. And so, after two days with the Indians, we start the trip downriver, and a completely different river it is, too, downstream from upstream, as we slide down the first rapid, bump through the second, and on, always following the smooth tongue of deep water into the boil of standing waves.

Somewhere in the woods around here, we are told, lives a white Indian tribe. No one has actually seen them. Could these be Riolama's people?

If the distance from Albina to Antecuma is roughly 300 km, and it took us 3 days to travel this distance upstream and, I am told, 2 ½ days downstream (each day consisting of approx. 9 hours) what is the average speed of our boat and that of the river? RT=D. An elemental math problem I've forgotten how to solve. It should be something like:

x = speed of canoe (km/hr)
y = " " river ( " " )
(x - y) 27 = 300 (upstream)
(x + y) 22.5 = 300 (downstream)

The Indians, Viano discovered, have stolen a large quantity of gasoline. Nevertheless, he has been impressed by the German-Indian boy and may take him on as a guide.

Dietmar: Those who speak compulsively of disaster may even wish for it and invite it, knowing it will satisfy them. While those around them suffer they can say, "Ah, did I not foresee this? Was I not correct?" Thus they derive their satisfaction.

A stop at Benzdorp, a one-horse town if there ever was one. A black gentleman, 65 yrs old, Fred Banfield by name, who's been here since 1938, a remarkably intelligent and well-informed man, sitting with his cane in the shade on a dilapidated porch, gave us the following info:

—In its heyday, Benzdorp produced about 250 kilos of gold a year. (The Belgian Congo produces 18 tons annually, he read somewhere.) Now the figure is ten kilos. Fifteen men still work back in the bush, a three-hour walk from here. Once there was a Dutch company and an American company, the Northshore Company of San Francisco. Both went broke.

"To finance a gold mine," Mr. Banfield says, "you need a silver mine."

—Surinamers are a worthless people. They'll never make anything out of their country. As soon as they get a little education, they want a desk job. For example, a man earning fifty guilders pays to have his son educated. When he is ready to work, the son turns down a job with a starting salary of seventy-five guilders. This, while the father, still earning fifty, supports him.

—God gives a man 3 score and 10 years. Mr. Banfield has five years left and is prepared to die at any time.

—Goldminers don't keep their earnings long. Whiskey and women. The old man chuckles when he recalls those times.

—There used to be a grove of bamboo by the riverbank where gold nuggets could be found with relative ease. Then the French police began to keep watch over the place, and you had to go at night, without a lamp, and, if you thought you had found a nugget you bit down on it to see if it was soft. Got to be there were more broken teeth than nuggets in that grove. The old man laughs again.

Mr. Banfield comes originally from Georgetown, where, incidentally, things are much better (meaning, I believe, that the blacks are now in charge), and speaks fluent English. The old fellow has a great deal of pride and declares finally he has never wanted to visit the United States, even if he could have afforded it, for blacks aren't welcome there. Look what happened to JFK, RFK and King, he points out, all of whom were for the blacks.

Our conversation took place in the sleepiest circumstances imaginable. The broiling sun, the sluggish river, the cock-eyed line of gray plank and palm shanties, rotting away but somehow still standing. Heavy mining machinery half-hidden along the edge of the jungle, rusting away, turning back into the soil. All contribute to an atmosphere of sodden tropical inertia in which the passage of time has been suspended for the past fifty years. Me, I was glad to get away from Benzdorp and feel the fluidity of the river lift the leaden weight of jungle torpor from my shoulders.

Before leaving we woke up the Chinaman who had, despite our arrival, just shut his shop for a siesta (11.30 AM), and drank beer and soft drinks in his house. Mr. Banfield says he gives NO CREDIT, not even for a shovel to go digging.

A sad, desperately hopeless but fairly benign *Heart of Darkness* kind of place.

M has adopted a baby bird called Pikimaati, or little friend (*pequeño* + mate?) that sits on the edge of its basket and squeaks to be fed every half hour. Chula eyes his little rival with suspicion. Shussing the foaming watery slopes, we safely descend Death on the Left, passing the wreckage of the other canoe less fortunate.

Dull green is the color of the jungle, a monotonous green.

You don't know a thing until you know the monotony of it.

An entire afternoon pelted by a driving, freezing rain. The sixth and last night spent in the school house on Grand Santi, tin-roofed and dry. A terrifying dream about the death of my father. I saw his soul running down a fence-line. It was a wolf.

Another encounter with Viano's sister, who had not finished complaining about the punishment meted out to her daughter. Another exchange of goods: sugar and corned beef for bananas, banana root, cassava bread, and tapioca root —"some to sell and some to hold."

*Bakru.* A man-made evil spirit, half wood, half alive. Fashioned like a doll with a human bone inside, it cannot be turned away from its diabolical mission.

I'm not the only one with bad dreams. A little boy in white pyjamas shook Jytta's hammock all night. An old woman with a stick and a big light around her head.

Recalling the days before the advent of outboard motors, Viano said that two men, constantly poling and paddling their canoe, took 16 days to reach Benzdorp. Thus did he learn the ways of the river. Yamaa will never know the river as he does. A powerful man, Viano, with a personality to match. The kind of guy you want on your side when an argument breaks out. Jytta, proud of her man, says again that nobody on the river has ever beaten him in a fight.

Having passed the last night on the river, we race downstream to catch the ebb tide that will hurry us to Albina.

The old woman who sweeps the village in the morning with

a palm frond has a filthy mouth.

The word on the river for cowry shell, with incredible appropriateness, is *pappamoney*—a name for which nobody here has an explanation. When I tell them that cowry shells were until recently used as currency in West Africa, the land of their ancestors, their eyes light up, all becomes clear. You see cowry shells worn as amulets by the old men of the river. I own a mass of cowry shells sewn into a belt which I bought from a Malian trader on the Djmaa el Fna in Marrakesh. It was once worth, I was told, twelve cows.

*Albina*

Mama feels "death beneath her feet." (For these people death comes from the ground.) She doesn't feel well, her skin hurts all over.

Everyone here, it seems, keeps birds. They carry them in cages wherever they go. But poor Pikimaati has died . . . Madeleine performs a touching burial service on the riverbank.

"Fishboy" was still in the water, head bobbing among the canoes. We threw him leftovers from the bank.

*November 21, back in Parbo*

I'm sitting in front of my typewriter on the balcony of this hotel, glass of whiskey in my hand, watching a colossal pink thunderhead turn ash white, like the face of a corpse, as the light drains from it. She's sitting cross-legged on the bed, doing her hair. That face-framing, just-brushed auburn hair provides enough bait for a lifetime's chase. Female entanglement to the dereliction of all else.

A load of mail at the American Consulate: more reviews of

*Tangier Buzzless Flies* from Athenaeum in New York and Secker & Warburg in London. A letter from Joe McPhillips in Tangier makes me homesick for Morocco. Dr. Kruesi writes again that x-rays confirm the early signs of emphysema. Even if I look after myself, give up cigarettes and stay out of smoky bars, is this the beginning of the end?

Last but not least, news from Tangier that Madeleine's Uncle Daan has taken a turn for the worse and is going to Amsterdam for treatment. She has promised her aunt to join them there so, just as we were about to settle into the Prime Minister's cabin, and I, primed to make a serious effort to complete the novel, this trip looks like coming to a crashing halt.

"This novel (*Under the Volcano*) then is concerned principally . . . with the forces in man which cause him to be terrified of himself." (Lowry)

And Virginia Woolf: "This vague and dream-like world, without love, or want, or passion, or sex, is the world I really care about."

If I knew exactly which world I cared about most deeply . . . Yet I do know, but am not prepared to contemplate that moment when all else must be set aside in order to achieve a uniquely creative life. I don't think she will be part of it, or wants to be. Ah, future decisions . . . I fear they will tear me up like paper. In my heart I am hoping I have sized up the situation falsely, but to go on, enduring this constant, dull pain. Ugh! I hope I'm wrong. As she herself points out, if this trip proves to be productive, who knows what the future will bring? Whose fault the indifference is may not matter—I simply can't live with it much longer. I'll probably end up sitting on the fence, just letting things happen as I've done all my life instead of taking decisive action.

I just want to be handled the way she handles her pet rabbits.

Lillian, the porcelain-skinned half-Chinese, half-Portuguese girl, who earned her law degree in the Netherlands, told us how the rich folks in Parbo amuse themselves.

When race riots are reported from Georgetown, ex-British Guyana, certain affluent citizens of Paramaribo fly by private plane which lands near the neighboring capital, whence they are able to reach with comparative safety an apartment building owned by a friend. Sipping gins and whiskeys on the penthouse balcony, they are able to observe the headhunting African rabble enter the Indian quarter. An Indian mob, screaming hysterically, quickly assembles and surges out, seeking revenge. An eerie glow cast by burning houses illuminates the scene . . .

Taxi driver: "Say the wrong thing and they call you in and make you full of holes, man."

*November 22*

Tomorrow—Thanksgiving. Lack of seasonal change numbs the passage of time. Except for our brief stay in high-altitude Mexico City, we have been travelling through the tropics ever since we entered Mexico, actually crossing the Tropic of Cancer near Mazatlán. October, November, December approaching—one month barely distinguishable from the next. Rainy season, dry season—is there a difference? Yet here in Paramaribo, just a few degrees above the equator, weather is cool, days are comfortable, nights long and sometimes passionate, albeit the whole venture I have come to find slightly, no, much more than just slightly, enervating. Ugh! Sometimes, I wonder, where has energy gone? Where compassion, patience, composure, faith and purpose? What about this book, that I can't seem to get on track?

The masts of a large freighter pass behind the palm trees and wooden buildings: the Surinam River is only a ¼ mile away.

*November 23*

We have decided, after a long conversation, to travel together as far as Belén in Brazil, and from there complete at least part of the most-looked-forward-to leg of this adventure—travelling by boat up the Amazon River from mouth to source— as far as Manaus. She doesn't need to be in the Netherlands for another two weeks, and can fly to Amsterdam from Manaus, via Caracas to help her Aunt Peggy care for her Uncle Daan and, hopefully, to see her daughter.

My so-called new ideas for the book turn out to be old ideas that have been before my eyes all this time. I've been groping around for a trail I never left. As Orwell wrote, "To see what is in front of one's nose requires a constant struggle."

The agonizing dilemma, when the person you love makes it impossible to love her. Who wishes to face the reality that love, like water dripping from a cracked pot during the night, has all but drained away? The precious liquid, never to be retrieved. The pot, which once appeared so sound, with many useful years ahead, the cherished pot, which never leaked a drop before . . . or had it? Would a flaw not have, under closer examination, been discerned long ago? Found that the pot was never meant to hold water at all, that it was just an ornament for display? This is a hangover talking.

Picked up my new suit today. Fits perfectly. She likes me in it, so that's a plus. We're invited out every night—bars, restaurants, people's houses . . . everybody wants to be with Madeleine. Her habit of flirting doesn't help. It may be harmless, but it hurts. Men leave messages at the desk proposing boat rides, jungle picnics, etc. I tear them up.

What also attracts attention from horny waiters and other lascivious gawkers is her gadget or "doodad." Madeleine, far-sighted, carries with her a platinum, diamond-encrusted, spring-operated mechanism which, when she slips it from its snakeskin sleeve and presses a button, flips itself erect with a little click—a pair of eyeglasses on the end of a stick which she uses to read the menu—her lorgnette.

*November 24*

Notes written in the Coconut Club Bar:
The dry wooden church, relic of the colonial era, stands alone in an empty field. The narrow steeple, desiccated like the arm of a woman grown old, beseeches shelter from the sky. The deserted church, built on pilings, windows broken, shutters hanging out. A pariah dog sleeps on the stairs, chickens wander underneath, and the grass has grown deep. It has been a long time since white Dutch people, seated securely within, lifted their hearts and voices to the Lord. But the steeple remains stiffly upright, the handmade star windows have been shattered, and the stars have gone out.

This derelict structure near the center of a teeming native village is not included in the life of the village. The high-pitched roof has never seen the snow for which it was designed. It stands indifferent to the babbling voices of the natives and the surge of their incessant, ant-like activity. Fashioned from native timber, the church stands rigidly aloof, mouldering toward oblivion. White people from a cold country brought with them this emaciated architecture, their bony idea of the spirit.

All have departed, except for those who linger in the adjacent field, where wooden crosses lean at crazy angles. Others have fallen and are turning back to the soil. The names of blue-eyed children, fair-haired people felled by malaria—their names are being erased by rain, fungus and the damp. They will not be remembered here. Not one cross stands upright; they are slowly being reclaimed by vines and ground creepers.

Madeleine passes slowly from cross to cross, looking for familiar names. She finds them—a great uncle, his wife and three small children, all dead within a week . . . yellow fever.

*Some Parbo characters:*

Madame Q, who seems such a pleasantly domestic Indian lady, turns out to be a compulsive gambler and something of a nymphomaniac. Her friends have become concerned, as she comes to them begging for loans to repay her gambling debts, which they know her husband will not reimburse. But, as her husband is an influential MP, they cannot refuse. And her sexual advances are becoming more frequent, vulgar and demanding. They are backed by ill-concealed threats, for her husband is a powerful politician.

Mister Rudy, of Lebanese descent, who invited us to his home to sample his mother's *rijstafel,* persists, to the amusement or dismay of his friends, in relating his numerous sexual adventures in Paramaribo and other capitals of the world.

"The best sex I ever had was in New York."

"There is electricity in the wires and in my veins."

"Tomorrow a 17-year-old is going to rape me. I met her in a shop. She can't keep her hands off me. We have a rendezvous at 4 PM."

In fact, nobody has ever seen him with a woman, and it appears that he cannot do without his mother, whom he still lives with, or without her excellent cuisine.

On his deathbed his father said: "Even though it's against the law, I want to leave everything to her. Look after her, son, but don't upset her. Everything is hers. She's the best I ever had."

*November 27, Belén, Brazil*

The airport scene at 4 AM resembled a murky set from Hieronymous Bosch. People were being herded in groups by heavily armed police across the ill-lit runway toward decrepit DC-4's, and to what unspeakable fate? We were obliged to skirt an enormous jet which, although empty, was revving its engines in the place where arriving passengers had to pass. Several among us lost hats, raincoats, umbrellas, and immigration visas in the howling kerosene gale. Chatting merrily, the ubiquitous customs officials automatically stamped any papers or documents that slid their way across the shiny, elbow-worn counter. Surly, exhausted passengers filed by like an old film strip.

This morning we were confronted with the usual crunch and thunder of thousands of ancient automobiles, battering the city into senselessness. This, after having been turned away by one hotel last night where our reservation requests were never received, we arrived at another and were given an unfurnished wooden box for twenty dollars. The hotel is located across the street from a fifty-storey office building in the process of construction. The workers arrived at dawn. Jackhammers set the tempo for superannuated buses whose mufflers have never seen a mechanic.

First glimpse of the mighty Amazon, and of the difficulties we will encounter to travel up the Great River. Quaint sternwheelers, steamers manned by pirate-like crews, all travelling our way but all, apparently, booked months in advance.

Towns like Belén (Bethlehem in Portuguese), with not a

self-confident, they will not deign to return a glance or even a lingering stare. Of the lean and wiry variety (not much flesh on those fellows), they operate in the field with no logistical support. (Little competition exists between the boys and the ladies. They work opposite sides of the street. Each knows who will come; each knows who is theirs.) A boy will lead the adventurous stranger to the grassy knolls of the park which, although just a few yards from the sidewalk, are completely obscured by shadows. There the willing victim is rolled and/or laid with a perfect view of the paseo, the kiosks, the newspaper vendors, the traffic jam, and the well-heeled ladies and gents on their way to the theatre.

This elaborately decorated Greek temple, whose solid red plush interior is bathed in golden light from spreading chandeliers, has opened its doors for an evening of classical music or other staid entertainment. The thuds and sighs from the bushes must surely be audible to the fancy folk passing by . . . there, a gentleman elegantly attired, emerging from a black limo, has tripped over a trousered leg which suddenly flipped from the grass onto the sidewalk. The trousers are unfashionably baggy, being gathered about the ankles. As the traffic signals change, a naked rump gleams red among the bushes. The man stumbles and grunts (from the bushes a series of curses and grunts responds) and hurries to catch up with his wife.

*November 28. Hotel Vanja (quieter) $38.00*

Ibis vendors, parrot vendors, and a vendor of turtles. The man who tried to sell us toucans yesterday turned up at our hotel this morning with a baby monkey in a wicker cage. They know an animal lover when they see one. I have to restrain Madeleine from acquiring a menagerie of sad, caged animals. Eureka! We have found passage to Manaus! And so tomorrow we shall set off westwards and northwards, ever so slightly, to the capital of Amazonia . . . 5 or 6 days. Madeleine will fly home to Amsterdam from there.

We hurried back to the river front to buy the well-made Brazilian hammocks. (The boys continued to hurl stones to bring down the green mangoes.) Then to the movies to see *Carnal Knowledge* in Portuguese. Then back to the hotel for a last shore-bound dinner in our room, for which I have promised a bottle of champagne.

She's quite a linguist, my Madeleine. Native Dutch, fluent English and French, good German, passable Spanish from a year spent on Mallorca, now Portuguese which she picked up in Mozambique. As we pass from country to country she displays a full range of fluency in these languages.

The thing about these high-born European girls who grew up in castles and stately homes, they haven't been to college, they haven't hung out in bars drinking beer with the boys. M will sip a *cachaça* (cocktail made of white rum* and cashew juice),but what she really craves is cold white wine or champagne. Try finding champagne in Amazonia, but after walking all over the city I did—a bottle of Chilean fizz on a dusty shelf in the back of a lantern-lit grocery store. It's cooling in an ice bucket on the bedside table while she packs and I write. Madeleine always packs my clothes as well as hers and says her mother told her one of her wifely duties was to shine her husband's shoes every night.

*4 AM (November 29)*

Can't sleep from anticipatory restlessness and excitement over the trip that begins tomorrow. Not only to Manaus but beyond: after Madeleine leaves a new kind of voyage must begin—one marked by deep solitude. Already I miss her, especially now, even before we have parted. Spray of auburn

*Also called *pinga, aguardiente* or *agua que passarinho nao bebe.* (Water the little birds won't drink).

hair on the snow-white pillow—she lies here asleep beside me while I prop this notebook on my knees and write by flashlight. Ought I to describe on these pages my love for her elusive, pained personality, a pain inflicted by myself, my love? And how do you explain to the one you love that the life of a writer is essentially a solitary one? An undeniable fact of life . . . my life.

The Amazon. World's biggest river. Not the longest, but with the most water in it. It drains an area about the size of the United States, from the snow-bound Andean peaks on the Pacific rim to the teeming mangrove swamps on the Atlantic. The mouth of the river is two hundred miles wide. An island in the mouth—Ilha de Marajó—is bigger than Belgium. When Pedro Alvares Cabral, the first Portuguese navigator to explore the coast off NE Brazil (first sighted on April 22, 1500), dipped a bucket into the sea and drank fresh water 500 miles from land, he knew he was onto something big.

*November 29, on board the*
AUGUSTO MONTENEGRO
HOLLAND SHIPBUILDING ASSOCIATION
AMSTERDAM YARD NO. 95 HOLLAND
AMSTERDAM DRYDOCK CY
AMSTERDAM*

At the speed of nine-and-a-half km/hr we plod upstream on this vast brown lake. Fringes of the rain forest barely visible about a mile off on either side. Scheduled stops: Breves, Gurupá, Almeirim, Prainha, Monte Alegre, Santarém, Obidos, Parintius, Itacoatiara and Manaus. Downstairs, in cattle class, swing hundreds of colorful hammocks; we are looking for a place to swing ours.

* Brass plaque over the bar.

Traumatic scene this morning, when the crusty old captain steadfastly refused to accept Chula on board, despite persistent entreaties from the young lieutenant, who had taken up our cause. The sight of M in tears had melted the young fellow's heart, but not that of the ornery critter on the bridge. Finally, just as it looked as if we might have to disembark with all our luggage, the problem was instantly solved by a nod in our direction from the president himself (of the steamship company), who had fortuitously come aboard to see off some friends. And so we are safely installed in our special class cabin, small but comfortable.

Will great thoughts be summoned up by this mighty river, god of waters? So far all I can make out on the riverbank are trees and more trees, strangling each other, swarming over each other as they stretch for the light. Others are dying, throttled, already dead. This dull green monotony has yet to inspire me. Where are the whispering monkeys, the giant sloth with his Mona Lisa smile, the dappled panther daintily balancing on a fallen log?

The beckoning canoes—the beseeching impoverished canoes that try to keep up. Some of the passengers throw down old clothes and pieces of bread. Abandoned sawmills and the rusting hulks of ancient river boats, villages and whole civilizations on stilts. Watery horizons—this could be an inland sea. Flocks of parrots in full flight and argument head home for the night. A flaming sunset over a river without banks.

By night, this ship with all its lights ablaze must appear from the shore like a floating birthday cake.

Around the turn of the century, a railroad was built, after several failures and appalling loss of life, connecting Porto Velho in Brazil with the rivers of Bolivia. I have just been told the line still functions.

The never-changing river bank—trees and more trees. Dull green, opaque, impenetrable—the tedious monotony of the jungle fills me with a stupefying torpor.

Already I feel an ache for the Andes. Thin air, space, clear vistas, bracing cold. Rid the lungs of this oppressive, dense phlegm, the color of which I care not to describe, except that it looks like some repulsive insect excretion. What noxious element is at work within my decrepit respiratory system, producing this gunk? I must watch over my health, as my mother insists and my doctor warns. I must take care of myself, as my father has been repeating for as long as I can remember. I must stop smoking. But what about my left hand which, whenever the penny drops sparking fresh ideas, compulsively creeps toward the Marlboro pack? And what about the smoky bars of Lima, Paris, Rome, Madrid, and Tangier where I learned to talk and think and learn and, ultimately, to write? Will my heart and head ever respond to the pleas from those who know better, let alone my lungs?

Miguel Ángel Asturias: a tense story *(The President)* crammed with extraneous detail and description that glue it all together.

We are transporting a shipload of ruffians—bushy, drooping mustaches, dark hooded eyes, long greasy hair, sallow pockmarked cheeks, striped T shirts and torn Levis. Drunk at ten o'clock in the morning. Cheap cigarettes, cheap booze, cheap women . . .

Our Man in Manaus: fellow with a nose like the pope's nose on the rear end of a chicken, speckled with black, crater-like pores. Sunken cheeks—he's lost all but a few teeth. Sallow, hairless cheeks. A sparse mustache smudges a thin upper lip. Shiny black hair, long bony fingers, a gap-tooth smile, obsidian beads for eyes. We leer at each other across the bar.

*December 1*

Last night, gauzy pink clouds foamed over the southern horizon. Cup of moon rose lobster red from bubble-gum-colored waters. Weird phenomenon—no explanation.

*Monte Alegre*

Red-tiled houses along the red clay street, church on the bluff above the river, where bells chime and firecrackers explode. Vultures congregate in groups along the shore, or wheel like dark predatory spirits over the town. Boys sell bananas, fish, mangoes, bread, manioc cookies, melons and obscene rubber sculptures. There's a baby monkey in the water. White herons, wading in a marsh, suddenly take flight. The ponderous flap of short, broad wings. Pink porpoises (*botos*) show their arched backs and dorsals. A flock of falcons whizzes by like jet fighters.

Each morning I dig out the grammar book and work for an hour or so on my Portuguese. But it's no good: I can't memorize these confounded endings and can't get my tongue around this Brazilian lingo. Much easier to cheat with Spanish. I close the book and return to reality, rubbing shoulders and clinking glasses with criminal types in the cattle-class bar.

A herd of water buffaloes. Brahmas and gauchos. M is excited.

*Santarem*

A Brazilian Ave Maria carried from the neon-lit cathedral to our ship anchored offshore. We passengers, prohibited by our testy captain from going ashore, although the ship stops for nearly two hours, sip beer by the rail, watch the glitter of carnival lights reflected upon the moving waters, and listen to the sweet notes of the Ave Marias and to the voices of the populace thronging the midway. Small craft—manned by sweating sinewy rowers wielding thick, crudely-carved oars; outboard-motor launches (motors of weird design, propellers on long, nearly-horizontal stems for use in shallow water—they must be a model manufactured 30 years ago in the U.S. or yesterday in Brazil. In fact they turn out to be Swedish). Slope-backed river craft ferry passengers and freight back and forth in the night. The waters of the Tapajos River—clear, black and sharply defined from the muddy Amazon.

*December 2*

Obidos, where we went briefly ashore to buy lemons to squeeze into our rum. Found no lemons but mangoes, pineapples and a bottle of *aguardiente* instead. At the outset of the return trip to the ship, which had dropped anchor a hundred yards offshore, our leaky and overladen canoe began to sink. Water poured in over the side and spouted up through a hole the size of a dime in the bottom. We would have gone down had it not been for the operator of the motor, a boy no older than seven, who summarily ordered two burly Brazilian soldiers dressed in battle fatigues over the side. So much water had come into the canoe that there was little difference between being in it and in the river. Shrieks of laughter when one of the soldiers was shocked by an electric eel. Another passenger began to bail with a broken calabash, and we made it back to the ship, where my *aguardiente* was confiscated by an unshaven member of the crew. (I had been warned—our ship is operated by the Brazilian navy.) So, the Ahab on the bridge has had his revenge.

Pink porpoises or dolphins, meanwhile, dive and play about the ship. A small fleet of canoes clusters about us, selling every species of jungle animal and bird, plus ugly half-dead river fish which resemble obsolete aquatic animals from the dinosaur age. Instead of scales, they own a hide like an armadillo's.

Vultures land on the red-tile roof of a warehouse, force the pigeons off, and spread their wings to dry in the sun. Another group of vultures chases the same flock of homeless pigeons from another roof, then spread their wings to announce their death-loving presence.

We are now passing through a skeleton forest of dead trees. What mysterious pestilence has defoliated them?

Only the spider knows how to move freely within her perfected web; all others get trapped. We have seen spider webs as broad as tennis nets, spiders the size of crabs . . .

A lesson I can't seem to learn: when you are in the company of a good-looking woman, avoid being bought drinks by South American men. While I was in the head, Madeleine took pity on a pair of toucans offered for sale. So now we have three birds in our tiny cabin, and Chula is jealous. If the Captain finds out, he'll toss us and them to the piranha.

*December 3*

Lunch. The woman sitting next to us on the communal bench saws off a piece of "shoe leather" (the mystery meat we have just been served). Staring at it on the end of her fork with an expression of mingled fascination and disgust, as though she had speared a cockroach, she forced it into her mouth and began to chew—slowly, long and hard.

My last bottle of rum, propelled by the dull pulse of the ship, is moving by itself to the edge of this table where I write.

A listlessness has come over me. All energy has departed. The past four days—I cannot separate one from another. The tedious green and brown monotony of the river has affected me soporifically. Have I ceased altogether to dream and to imagine?

The tiny farms along the river bank, the half-naked people who watch speechless as the ship chugs by. The wretched aspect of their stilted dwellings, the impenetrable and inhospitable gloom of the forest behind them, this sluggish dull brown river—all fill me with a stupefying torpor. Something within me rebels against listlessness and all its relations—the heat, the starchy food, the heron waiting motionless by a pool of water, the monotonous inactivity of life aboard ship, the absurdly slow pace as it creeps upriver—ugh!—but with all this time on my hands, instead of rousing myself to a productive mood, I have slumped toward apathy, dreaming of mountain streams.

We sweat. Each movement produces and reproduces successive films of sweat that cover the entire surface of our bodies. I take showers. We nap, sometimes together, sometimes apart. I read. I study Portuguese. She writes letters and talks to the birds. The timid, half-tame toucans—Heckle and Jeckle, I call them—hop lightly around the cabin like blithe forest spirits. The oversized, canoe-shaped beaks—not heavy, I think they're hollow—deftly cut up the bananas and other soft fruit she gets from the ship's cook.

According to Indian legend *(The Raw and the Cooked,* by Claude Lévi-Strauss) the toucan flattened its beak trying to break the shell of a terrapin. The woodpecker succeeded. "Then the birds painted themselves with the red blood, the blue fluid from the gall bladder, and the yellow fat. The toucan smeared blue all around its eyes, and yellow on the end of its tail, and a band of yellow across its breast. It also put a daub of blood on its tail."

I pace the deck, trying to fix my mind on work, but what I see is green mud and brown water. What I feel is the damp. What I smell is the vegetal stink of new life stubbornly emerging. What I hear is the interminable dull pulse of the ship. What I taste is the aftertaste of beer and manioc and rice. And yet ... it's been a good trip. Without knowing exactly what they will be, I am laying down the ground rules, the terms and time under which the novel will be rewritten. Tomorrow . . . Manaus! As we approach this mythic jungle capital, I feel the same twinge of anticipatory excitement that Joe McPhillips and I experienced when we trucked across the Spanish Sahara toward Smara, Michel Vieuchange's forbidden city.

Madeleine and I shared a tiny bottle of Cointreau *muito savroso* which, like this trip, quickly came to an end. We clung to each other through the night to ward off the reality that she will be leaving the day after tomorrow.

*December 4, Manaus*

Good Lord—skyscrapers! What has happened to the sleepy, romantic riverine town of my imagination? The Japs got here ahead of us. They've taken over. Smokestacks. Pollution. Traffic jams.

*December 5. Hotel Amazonas $80.00*
*Restaurant Canto de Alvorada*
*" Chapeau de Palha*

Tomorrow she leaves. Solitude looms heavy and long. A dark shadow cast by the impending vacuum. If this is what I have secretly desired and openly needed, how to explain the expanding hollowness within? The disquieting hollowness. Have I lost my nerve? Am I weary of travel? Or is it that I have found neither peace nor excitement in these tropic lands, have learned nothing profoundly, have not been moved? Like my character Mi Amigo Maxwell in *Tangier Buzzless Flies*, I seem to understand less every day.

The accumulation of experiences, these unique travel experiences, fragments of which I attempt to record, seem to have obscured the clear picture I once thought I had of myself. For the first time in my life, I want the mountains. I need another form of desert, where vistas are clear, the air dry, the sky vast. I'm sick of mud. Let the Andes come on with a rush!

*11 PM*

Tragedy. While we were out of the hotel having supper last night, the Brazilian maid came into our room, turned down the beds and thoughtlessly sprayed the place with some heavy-duty insecticide. When we returned we found both toucans dead. Chula, locked in the basket, looked woozy but somehow survived.

This kind of thing is happening all over Brazil, all over the world.

After initial tears and anger, Madeleine, who believes implicitly in the natural order of things, carried the feathery corpses downstairs, marched into the office of the thousand-apologies hotel manager, then dropped them into the alligator pond outside the front door. A splash and a gleam of lizard armor and the toucans were gone.

*December 6*

Our last day together. A Polaroid photo in the park which I scotchtape into this notebook. We taxied out of town for a swim in the Rio Negro. The Amazon carries millions of tons of sediment washed from the slopes of the Andes—thus its muddy brown color. The Negro, rising in the swamps of Venezuela, bears an emulsion of decayed vegetal matter, producing tannin, which tints the water brownish-black—thus its name. Like swimming in tea. Below the confluence of these two mighty rivers, the division of waters is visible for miles.

We visited the zoo where we saw our first—I hope last—anaconda. About 30 feet long it lay motionless on the grass, its life being slowly drained away by a legion of blood-sucking ticks.

The airport scene. On the blazing runway we hugged for the last time this year in a crowd of sweating, shouting, kiss-blowing Brazilians. She flew off to Caracas where she will spend the night before catching the big jet to cool Amsterdam, while I . . . face the prospect of travelling up this hot, sluggish, mosquito-blown river. Alone.

*4 PM*

I lie on the white hospital bed in this white hotel room, next to the imprint so recently made by her body, reading a Gideon's Bible in Portuguese, trying to banish the black thoughts of guilt and loneliness from my soul. Alone in Amazonia . . . I even miss Chula.

*About 5 PM*

Like some huge reptile, a dank, antediluvian gloom slithers from the river and wraps its coils about the city. This is heavy air, rank with the stink of the swamp. Ah, for a glimpse of the Med, with clear light glinting off swinging wave-ends, I would willingly trade my hammock, my mosquito net, even my machete.

A heavy dream last night in which I had been accused, in a series of written threats, of plagiarising the so-called "Roof Theory" of a famous writer. A Kafkaesque noose of guilt tightened about my neck. I could no longer be certain whether I had or had not committed this terrible crime, until it dawned on me that nobody ever bothered to read my books. The dream lasted all night, or so it seemed. I woke drenched with sweat and lay on the bed in a daze, listening to the tropic rain hammer the city.

An island, shaded by towering mango trees, where I went this morning for a beer, occupies the center of the divided cobbled avenue. Here, for all the relentless crunch and thunder of traffic, a comparative silence reigns. From a large kiosk, its roof flaring out into broad eaves supported by lacy iron girders, for all appearances constructed at the same time as the famous theatre on the hill, beer is served. Tables and chairs have been set out under a tiled roof pavilion. Nearby stands a low, brick, box-like structure, whose odor has rendered one side of the pavilion most disagreeable—the public latrine.

The clientele—strictly men, all Brazilians, all speaking Portuguese. From the diversity of human faces present—black, white, Asian and multiple variations upon these themes—you'd think every nation in the world must have its representatives here.

In Brazil one frequently encounters dark-skinned people with disconcertingly clear eyes. These eyes must be evidence that a white man slipped into his bloodstream somewhere along the line and has been trapped. From the face of the African, the eyes of the white man look out— fearful, caged and resigned, confidence lost long ago.

On the whole, a gregarious, beer-drinking lot, although there are those, as one is apt to find in any café, who are alone.

They sit quietly before their glasses and stare off into space, absorbed by their own thoughts. Like me.

*December 8*

Laundry Brazilian-style. To identify my clothes for the laundry, the maid sews my name in red thread into each item. A neat job of embroidery. I do not know if she is the evil one who murdered our birds.

This hotel, surrounded by the alligator-filled moat, sits at the top of Oswaldo Cruz park. From my third-floor balcony I can gaze across at the cathedral and beyond, to the Rio Negro, where the big ships drop anchor and wait to discharge their cargo. Vultures wheel and soar above the dock area, where the cranes dip and swing as gracefully as their feathery namesakes. Through the dense foliage of the mangoes, I can just make out the iron roof of the kiosk.

About 6 PM, after the gloom had set in, having lain all afternoon in bed reading *Heart of Darkness*, I walked in a somber mood down to the cathedral. While pretending to pray, teenage schoolgirls looked boldly about them. The backs of their uniforms were soaked through with sweat. Women with skirts clinging to their buttocks went down on their knees. I enjoyed the coolness of the church for a while, and said the usual prayers in an attempt to purge my soul of Conrad's black and heavy themes of sex and death. Then I went to the kiosk for a beer.

Peripatetic shoeshine boys, vendors of candy and cigarettes, beggars, and aimless children circulate among the tables. (The beggars are periodically driven off by the harassed, exhausted waitresses.) After dark, the prostitutes circle with the deliberate, impassive persistence of vultures.

The shoeshine man, whose elaborately decorated stand is next to the kiosk, has become something of a friend. João is his name. He blithely charges me 3 cruzieros for a shine, when the price all over town is 2.

He holds the key to the public latrine.

"Cost you fifty centavos to take a leak in there, boss. Piss in the park if you don't want to pay, but you'll be taking a chance as well. There's a law against it, and if the police . . . "

At that moment a VW squad car pulled up to the curb. Two young muscular cops in berets jumped out and grabbed hold of a youth—apparently a deserter from the army. They dragged him off, yelping.

The shine process: a quick preliminary brush to eliminate superficial dust and dirt. Water and alcohol applied with a toothbrush. Another quick brush. Polish put on with another worn-down toothbrush. Another brushing. Second layer of polish rubbed on with the finger. Shifting to the next shoe, he repeats the process. Each shoe is then rerubbed with a finger until the polish has sufficiently dried to make the finger squeak. A final brush and rag, and the job is done.

João also does shoe repairs. Passing at a distance, I saw him bent over in hunched concentration, cutting a sole from a sheet of leather. Or hammering on a lady's shoe, while a fat brown painted creature occupied his stand, dangling a plump bare foot in mid-air.

The green tiles on the Teatro Amazonas coldly reflect the light like the scales of an anaconda. A certain atmosphere of cosmopolitan decadence radiates from the theatre and the cafés around the Plaza, where I hear Arabic spoken by Lebanese and Syrian traders.

I took in two Grade B Brazilian films,

1. *Bangbang Violento*
2. *Betty: Alta*
   *Fria*
   *Loca,*

walked the wavy mosaic sidewalks, spent money and wrote postcards.

The currency of this country is in a terrible state. Banknotes so long in circulation they've become as ragged and fragile as autumn leaves, so filthy and greasy you recoil from the touch. So few coins in circulation that you regularly receive change in kind—chewing gum, candy, postage stamps. And the postage stamps come without glue. It's a hassle with the paste wheel at the Post Office.

*December 9. Restaurant Xodo*

This city is the victim of ruthless economic takeover by the Japanese, whose goods—machines, motorcycles, every kind of electric, photographic, and optical equipment—spill from the shops onto the pavement. There is barely enough time to uncrate them before they are snapped up by hordes of acquisitive citizens who arrive daily on special shopping flights from Brasilia, Rio, and São Paolo.

Manaus abounds in drugstores. In Mexico City it was oculists; in Panama, shoeshops. Here there's a drugstore on every corner. Brion Gysin once remarked that the excessive number of pastry shops being opened in Tangier signalled a certain feminization of the city headed for decline and disaster.

I am being followed. He has the scruffy blond beard and washed-out blue eyes of a missionary. Aimlessly he wanders these streets, like the lost souls he has been sent out to save. I first passed him as I came out of the Post Office. Our eyes met. At the corner I bumped into him again, hurrying from the opposite direction. He must have run all the way around the block to meet me. Dirty white shirt out at the waist, faded dungarees. In a photographer's shop where I had gone to buy postcards, I looked up: there he was. At a shoeshop where I had made inquiries about the availability of Dr. Scholl's footpads, I saw him loitering outside, reflected in the window. Eventually I was able to shake him, but I think he knows where my hotel is and may be waiting downstairs. I began to feel sorry for him, until I spotted him lurking in the background of a photo I had taken of myself in the park. This guy is giving me the creeps.

I have just woken from a too-long siesta and cruel dream. Some divine creatures were attempting to make themselves known to us. They sailed overhead on transparent flying carpets. We saw the marks of their space vehicles in the sand. We heard their laughter. They were tall, slim elegant young people, and they were immortal. They wanted to meet us and tell us their secrets . . . Then, abruptly, I received the news that Madeleine was not in Amsterdam as I had thought, that she had not even made it as far as Caracas. Her plane had crashed and all the passengers had frozen to death in the Andes. (An image inspired by the Chilean disaster I had read about in the newspapers.) I was hysterical, smashing things, breaking everything in sight with a police billy, screaming "Murderers!" at the airline people. A cop was approaching, about to arrest me, when I woke up.

A flag with the motto *Libertad y Orden* hangs limply over the door of the Ecuadorian Consulate across the street.

João spits. "One wishes," he said, pointing an angry finger at a twenty-storey building going up, "for a little more of the latter

*(Orden)* at the top, among those who are mucking with our world for profit and pleasure, and for more of the former *(Libertad)* at the bottom, for those of us who wish to take advantage of our remaining days to, ah, provide some liquidity to the situation."

His friend, who occupied a low bench beside him—he suffers from hernias—nodded enthusiastically.

An antique truck rumbles by, loaded with sacks of flour. Sitting astride the sacks are three or four muscular powdered individuals with empty flour sacks tied about their heads and flowing across their shoulders, looking for all the world like a group of rugged, dusty Arabs.

A boy no more than six approached my table. A filthier lad I had never seen. Black bare feet and brown teeth, his whole body was covered with dirt. He had long straight eyelashes, like the weighted eyelashes of a doll which open and close when you rock it. To my amazement, he whispered in my ear, *"Bakshish."* Then he proceeded to bite himself and showed me the teeth-marks. He pinched himself and showed me the pinch-mark. He had a sweet smile. Then he bit my finger and showed me the marks. Sharp little teeth like a puppy's. He scratched me with his dirty little finger nail and giggled. Then he held out his dirty little hand and asked again for money.

She had huge dark eyes and smooth coffee-colored skin. No more than eight. Giggling, she poked me in the ribs and felt in my pocket for loose change. Then she went away. A minute later, I spotted her on the sidewalk, grinning. When she knew she had my attention, she stuck out a long pink tongue, so long that the end of it touched her chin. With a forefinger she stroked the dazzling pink groove of it.

Brushes churn over my shoes, a smoking cigarette butt balances on a tin can. The key to the public latrine is João's most valued possession. All his life he has worked in this beer garden across from the Cathedral Park. Only beer is served, in large green bottles. Beer drinkers, it is well-known, must urinate a great deal, and the public latrine is conveniently located beside the beer garden, beneath the mango trees. João has worked and fought for the key all his life.

"With this," he says, holding up the key, which has a bit of wood attached to it by a wire, "I don't have to work hard anymore. With this, my life is better and longer. With this, I have been able to feed and clothe not only myself but the whole family. And let me tell you, boss, the family is big! This —this is the key to life!"

As he spoke, one of the drinkers rose solemnly from a table, stumbled toward us with the gait of a sleepwalker, let fall a coin upon the plate, took the key and headed for the latrine.

"Don't look a monkey in the eye," counselled his friend, the one with the hernia. "It makes him mad."

At the Peruvian Consulate my visa was issued, in the absence of the consul, by the live-in janitor. Leaning on his broom in front of an open closet where I made out the corner of an unmade bed, he asked with a sly grin if there is anything else he could do for me . . .

Ah, for the booming Pacific, for sunlight reflected off cold water, for the taste of salt air, saltwater . . . saltwater fish! To swim against an undertow, to dive beneath the spilling combers, to be rolled under and to surface gasping for breath, salt spray and spume flying!

¿COMO SOMOS?
¡CROMOSOMOS!

*December 10. Parador Ticuna $34.00*

Leticia, Colombia, where 3 countries meet—Colombia, Peru, and Brazil. Came here by plane from Manaus—a hair-raising flight on an unpressurized DC3 dodging titanic crackling thunderstorms over the endless carpet of rain forest.

Another sleepy riverine town. Hammock time. 3,000 miles from its mouth, the Amazon here is still a mile wide, swifter and full of tree wreckage washed from the flooded forests of Peru. The cages of sad animals, mostly monkeys, bound for laboratories in the U.S., are piled on the wharf. Saddest of all, the giant otter whines and squeaks in loneliness.

Black vulture lumps stud the distant, naked branches . . . water birds take flight over the swamp, their broad wings reflect on the silvery silent lagoons . . . eerie cries echoing my solitude. Flocks of Chulas fly home for the night, chattering excitedly among themselves. Now our Chula's with his mistress (and mine) far away on a cold continent . . .

A meteorite disintegrating in a flash of green light is reflected upon the flowing waters of the Amazon.

*Benjamin Constant, Brazil*
*December 11. Bar Très Nacòes*

Crossed the Amazon by water taxi (dugout canoe) on a sentimental pilgrimage to this collection of shacks on sticks. Although not directly named for him, what would the author of *Adolphe* and lover of Madame de Staël have made of this stilt town whose main street is a splintering boardwalk a few inches above the stagnant swill of swamp water?

Lost in the swamp: with one inch or less of freeboard, forced to bail constantly with a calabash the water which slipped in over the side, vulnerable to any stinging snake or other biting creature we might disturb, we strenuously paddled the fragile dugout canoe through the thick vegetation of the flooded forest. The water, invisible until the weed has been parted by the paddle, hides, my guide tells me, piranha and caimans. The weed swarmed with insects. I could not lay a hand on a leaf without a small army of them marching aboard my arm. Contact with the canoe brought them over the side in legions. Clouds of mosquitoes whined about our ears. Hairy vines swatted our faces. Black spiders the size of my hand dropped from the trees into the canoe. They were tremendously fast, they bit, and they had to be killed instantly. Any sudden movement required to do so, or even to avoid one, invariably brought a new torrent over the side, bearing another host of water bugs.

Odorico, my native guide, happily allowed us to become lost or trapped in the weeds, which he had earlier described as a black-water lagoon where pink dolphins play. He forgot to paddle and chuckled to himself over the prospect of a canoe loaded with fish.

*"Hay mucho pescado, meester."*

Indeed the swamp so teemed with fish that he only had to throw an iron-tipped cane spear blindly into the khaki-colored water. A klunk meant that it had skewered yet another prehistoric creature, with a hide like an armadillo's.

"Are there snakes around here, Odorico?"

*"Si, hay mucho, meester."*

"Piranha?"

*"Claro, meester. Plenty."*

"Well, row, damn it! Let's get the hell out of here!"

In the recesses of the weed-choked lagoon, strange vulture-like birds could be seen hopping from branch to branch of a dead tree, hooting mournfully. Intrepid black weavers mocked our plight by imitating engine noises.

*Restaurant Bar La Barra*

Character for the novel: Tall, thin balding man about 40, in need of a shave. Like some seedy character created by Damon Runyon, he has a slight stoop, a protruding Adam's apple, and he speaks softly out of the side of his mouth. A stained, hand-made, half-smoked cigarette droops from the other. Large luminous eyes always rotating, alert to what's going on in the bar. Oops, he has just reappeared clean-shaven. He has a long nose. Something distinctive, sympathetic and vulnerable about his razor-nicked face. From behind the scenes he controls everything.

Bottles of rum, pisco and whiskey sit on shelves behind the bar; opposite stands a display refrigerator loaded with cabbages and eggs. The fat lady up front presides over a bevy of pretty Indian waitresses.

Back at the hotel the maid sings as she makes up my bed: *"Yo no soy marinero . . ."*

Back at the bar after a quick shower, a conversation with a Brazilian river captain. Belén to Benjamin Constant: 30 days up, 20 days down.

He and his friend are flattered when I comment that Brazil is beginning to have the same problems as the U.S.

*"Ombrigado, senhor, muito ombrigado."*

To them pollution is a sure sign of progress.

*December 12, Iquitos, Peru*

The Amazon at high water. The flood rips off whole sections of the bank. Great trees fall booming into the river, dragging others, vine-connected, and slowly get underway as the current grips them. Masses of driftwood come curling downstream to hang up on some sand bar or shallow place. The upstream points of all the islands and sandy spits are cluttered with tree wreckage from the forest. Branches shake, bend, and snap back as the current tries to pry them loose. White limbs of dead trees are lined with green parrots. Shiny coils of marooned reptiles loop the upper branches.

Missionary-type in the Iquitos airport sent here from some place like Salt Lake City to stir up mischief among the Indians: lean, blond, close-shaven (shiny face), short-cropped hair, light khaki clothes, sandals, tattooed forearms, beady blue eyes. He totes a thin sinister black briefcase containing the word of God. His.

*December 12, Pucallpa*

Hotel Mercedes $3.30 where I am surrounded by a crowd of Americans here to shoot a film about a plane crash in the jungle. The sole survivor was a four-and-a-half year old girl. She lived with the animals for a while, followed a stream, and walked out of the forest.

I am afflicted, for the second time in less than a month, with jungle lice. One welt the first night breeds dozens the second. The cooties bury themselves under your skin and proceed to lay eggs, which hatch and travel (via the capillaries, I suppose) to new territory. All itch horribly. Gasoline doesn't slow them down.

*Pucallpa waterfront on the Ucayali River:*

Name of boat: YOU SEE ME SUFFERING YOU LEAVE ME CRYING
Restaurant: CHICKEN, LIZARD AND PIG—WE RESUSCITATE THE DEAD IN WHICH LIFE ONCE WALKED

Mountains of wild boar skins bound for the shoe factories of Hamburg. Ocelot, deer, monkey, snake: I am glad Madeleine is not here to see this shameful bounty of wholesale slaughter in the forest. Nobody gives a damn and nobody will, until the trees have been cut down and burned and the animals wiped out. Then it'll be too late.

A boy walks down the street with an elephant toad on a leash; in the other hand he holds a bright green lizard.

Intrepid vultures, tame as chickens, strut in gangs down main street. Heads and necks covered by coarse black leathery scales. You have to shoo them out of the way.

I have found a postcard showing a building here in Pucallpa which looks exactly like a square Moroccan mosque tower. While searching for it I learned that it was torn down some years ago by Canadian priests. My waiter, the one who told me about it, is called Abdelsalam.

*December 13, Tingo Maria. Hotel Las Turistas $19.00*

I can hardly believe I'm back in this place that Joe McPhillips and I first visited in 1959, again in 1960 and 1964, lured by the dream of starting up a coffee plantation in the Peruvian jungle. The dream may have been coffee, but the result—for me—was a writing career. It was in this room, which I specifically requested, and at this very same wooden table, I think, where I began keeping this diary 13 years ago.

Neither this picturesque riverside hotel nor the high jungle town with its grass airstrip has changed at all. Sadly the most notable personalities—Giacomo and Max Lovatelli, Laszlo Karolyi, David, et al—the eccentric and colorful European coffee planters who showed us so much hospitality—have long since departed.

I pace the well-oiled hardwood deck of the hotel; I tread the high pitted road into town. At the place on the Huallaga riverbank where I boarded, all those years ago, a balsa raft for a week's swirling, thundering adventure in the Peruvian wilderness, with only Juan and Osorio, my two rivermen, as companions, I scan the river while vultures alight on the boulders beside me with "a dry rush of wings." (Bill Burroughs—he stayed in this hotel when he came here in the '50's looking for the hallucinogenic drug *yage,* a.k.a. *ayahuasca* or *la viña de la muerte.*) All around are the dark forested hills, once so familiar, with clouds clotting about their summits. The flow of Huallaga fills the night with a soporific rush. On the other side of the road, the town generators pound, as they have always done.

For old times' sake I followed my guide hacking his way through the jungle to what was once Giacomo and Mary Ann Lovatelli's coffee farm. They didn't have much money, no meat on the table, only *ronsocco*—river pig (capybara) which Giacomo hunted at night in the swamp—rice and the fiery hot peppers which Joe munched like carrots. He had a mouth lined with asbestos.

Their *finca* had subsided into ruin, the land reclaimed by the jungle. The coffee trees dead, throttled by vines. The old timer told me, "Even bananas won't grow here any more." Their beautiful thatched, hand-made wooden house by the river nothing but a couple of termite-riddled walls, everything else having fallen down or been carried off by the natives. The drive to the farm was overgrown and passable only to a man on foot, if he had a machete. Gone the laughter, the European gaiety and sophistication. Departed, all of them—*"debiendo al banco mucha plata."* The river will never hear again the sound of Italian, Hungarian, or French being spoken at the cocktail hour. Giacomo thundering into town in his Land Rover, leaping out to grab a poisonous snake by the tail and whirling it above his head until it was dizzy. The insane and not-so-harmless practical jokes, with poor Laszlo usually the butt, like putting a dead bushmaster in his bed, which turned out to be not-so-dead.

Mary Ann, Giacomo's American wife, told me the story when, alone on the farm, she was shaken awake by an Indian servant who told her she must leave the house immediately. The army ants were on the march. She got her baby out just in time and waited by the river while her house was invaded by millions of voracious insects. The army ants are a blessing in disguise, she told me, as they go through the thatched roof and clean the house of every roach and rodent that does not have the sense or ability to flee. But she was fortunate to have been warned, for she had heard of other cases in which neglected infants had been found dripping with ants.

And Laszlo, the eternal hunter, wading up to his neck in the river, holding rifle and ammo out of the water, watching helplessly while his elusive prey, the black panther, smiled at him from the riverbank and vanished into the forest before he had a chance to get off a shot . . .

*December 14*

An except from that early diary:

*September 16, 1959*

Arriving back at the Hotel Touristas after driving

around the jungle all day with Diegas, the local bank manager, looking at coffee plantations for sale, we found young Carlos Futenechet waiting for us in his jeep. We immediately turned around and headed out to his plantation for the night.

Carlos is only 17 yet runs the family coffee plantation, or *finca,* single-handed. His father recently died, a terrible tragedy for the family, and his mother is in Lima trying to sell the place. Miles out in the jungle, it took 2 hours to get there.

We arrived after dark—Joe, myself, Carlos and Carlos's man Friday, called Bolivar. On the way through the coffee trees we stopped at the huts by the track where Carlos gave instructions to the workers for the next day. They respect his judgement and took their hats off while they talk. This man, or boy, seemed to have everything under control. He has had to assume, at an early age, more responsibility than either Joe or I have ever dreamed of.

When he cut the motor in front of the hacienda the jungle closed in, and we were serenaded by the shrill scream of tropical insects. Entering the small, poor, but tidy house, Carlos introduced us to the rest of the family—Edie, 19 years old with dirty blond hair and deep brown eyes, Hendrica 15, Heidi 2, and baby Peter 7 months, sick, with running sores all over his body. Heidi and Peter were naked, Edie and Hendrica in patched and faded dresses you could almost see through. All went barefoot. They are of Swiss-German origin, but their skin had taken on a distinctly yellow pallor from the malaria dope all consume.

We were touched by the hospitality of this Swiss Family Robinson, but could not help feeling sorry for them. Isolated in the jungle, they were obviously lonely, especially Edie. They had spent their entire lives on the farm. Home-educated, whatever that means, they had never been to school.

Before dinner Carlos poured out shots of pisco, showed us the skins of boa constrictors he had killed, and gave us some data on the farm: it is divided into 3 sections—El Carmen, Victoria, and Helvetia. He admitted that the farms are pretty run down, due to lack of capital. With fresh investment this could be a fine *finca*, for the coffee is of high quality.

Carlos said: they own 500 hectares of which 110 are in coffee. These produce from 8 to 12 quintals of coffee per hectare which they sell at 910 *soles* per quintal. The land is valued at about 3000 *soles* per hectare including everything and yields about 8000. Adding all this up, they should clear about 500,000 *soles* or approximately $17,000 per year. And yet they still owe the bank 700,000 *soles*. It doesn't make sense. I don't think they are producing as much coffee as they think they are. The banker Diegas says that as far as he knows they only produced 240 quintals last year. Not much for a farm this size. Raising four kids is a heavy responsibility. One ought to be a bachelor to start out in coffee.

Dinner: red beans, rice and *ronsocco* that Carlos shot the day before, served by Edie. She glided around the table barefoot, a kind of sultry animal presence. Except for a couple of trips to Lima, she'd never been out of Tingo, never been off the farm, never been on a date. Her dress looked as though it had been stitched from burlap sacks, now linen-like from repeated poundings on river rocks. A wave of riverine odor, of one who has bathed soapless in fresh water all her life, followed her about the room.

They are in the clutches of the banker Diegas, the one who showed us around. He beats his American wife with a stick, according to Carlos. The woman is so abject she has not learned a word of Spanish, even though she's been in Tingo more than ten years.

Going back to Diegas, in addition to trying to sell us various failing coffee plantations, he made us another offer. He personally owns 1000 hectares "outside of town." On this he claims 500 hectares of wild rubber trees are growing. As yet this land is undeveloped since there are no roads in or out. ("Outside of town," we have learned, means way the hell out in the jungle.) However, a road is being built "in the general direction" and should be completed "in a year or so." Then it would take a four-hour jeep ride followed by a four-hour canoe trip down river to reach his property. How you get back he didn't say. Frankly, I don't believe he's ever been to the place.

He would make a deal with us if we went in and took out the rubber. He would lend us 250,000 *soles* to get started. Now rubber is potentially the best crop. Once you get it into production your worries are practically over. However, it takes 8-10 years for a cultivated rubber tree to start producing. His property already has thousands of mature wild trees that simply need to be tapped. Wild rubber brings in 14 soles/kg while the cultivated is worth 19 soles. Our best bet would be to go in there to tap and start cultivating trees at the same time. It should be hugely profitable. Also rubber requires a small labor force.

We did not discuss specific terms of the deal, but Diegas gave us a note to a man in Lima who would give us an option on an additional 500 hectares of rubber land "outside town." This whole idea of farming in the Peruvian jungle is beginning to sound more and more harebrained . . .

*December 15*

*Las Cuevas de las Lechuzas* The damp, dripping walls of the jungle cave reverberated with the growlings and grindings of thousands of barn owls, or whatever nocturnal birds they might be. Maybe vampire bats. The ground, I discovered—to my disgust—teemed with black beetles—dung devourers who feed upon the bird droppings, which must be several feet deep. Another cockroach-like insect, resembling a trilobite which, at the first sign of danger (me), burrowed into the dung.

Upon returning to the hotel, I now read an official notice from the Ministry of Agriculture, warning that the caves are saturated with mushrooms that cause a condition technically known as histoplasmosis, a hole-in-the-lung-making-disease, whose action upon the human organism produces *trastornos de gravidad* (serious disturbances). The university has isolated it, and is now looking for an antidote, but until it finds one—STAY OUT. Now that I think of it, the cave opening resembled a gigantic maw, with one colossal stalactite hanging down in the recesses, like an obscene tonsil.

This weakness that is like death. This fatigue that is like death. These trees—I have seen too many of them. I do not think I have the energy to cut a single one of them down. The endless repetition of hot, sweaty days—eating, sleeping, dressing, shaving—often seems dreary beyond words. Brown water flows down from the hills, black water from the swamps. These rivers—they flow and flow; they will never cease flowing. The green canopy covers and devours all. I am beginning to find the jungle enervating and tiresome, and will be glad to leave it.

*December 16. By collectivo taxi ($2.50) to Huanuco in the foothills of the Andes. Hotel Turistas ($7.40)*

Good to see eucalyptus trees again. And cactus and cane brakes and fig trees and these dry mud walls. The rammed mud technique used here is identical to the one still employed in Morocco, including our adobe house among the palm trees of the Marrakesh oasis. It was a skill brought to the New World by the newly-Christianized Moors. I look out upon red tile roofs and naked hillsides, smell the dust, and think of greater Andalucia which once included Morocco and southern Spain. Calla lilies in bloom. So good to walk the cactus lanes and breathe the dry air. My lungs and spirit need more space than the jungle can provide.

Name of my Andean truck: SOLO CONTRA EL DESTINO

*Still in Huanuco*

The road to Cerro de Pasco was blocked by a *huaico*, or mud slide, so we had to come back here for the night. A *huaico* is a frightening sight: a torrent of thick brown mud with the consistency of liquid cement, churned by some rainstorm up in the mountains, was pouring out of a gully in huge waves. Within minutes, a veritable sea of mud had covered the road to a depth of 10 feet. Undulating eerily, like some science fiction horror, nothing can stop its progress. Moving with viscous imperturbability, it will carry buses and trucks before it. Can't leave this place until the rain lets up and the *huaico* stops *"trabajando."* Then the bulldozers can go to work. There have been so many of these *huaicos* lately as to warrant an editorial in *El Commercio*.

And so, after twelve years, Huanuco. Walking beside a river

bed, whose banks are overgrown with cactus and eucalyptus, I feel the sun hot on my back. I am searching for an Inca ruin. The clarity of air, a true blue sky, the dry stone walls, the rushing stream reflecting sunlight in bright points, the round brown hills have filled me with a nostalgia for my home in Morocco.

An Indian woman in the *collectivo* admired my Panama hat. I took a meal in a Chinese restaurant (Chifa Confort, teléfono 2405). Along with my bill the grinning oriental presented me with a pocket calendar for 1973.

Something so heartbreakingly sweet and gentle and fragile and hopeless about these mountain Indians. The young men, with their beardless cheeks and shocks of straight black hair, look no older than boys. And the women, some of them so pretty, with clear skin smooth like fine porcelain, their doll-like children with bright pink cheeks and huge solid black eyes.

As a race, they've got it all together; yet they appear to have nothing. They are a people possessed of such a variety of contrary characteristics—boundless energy and implacable inertia, bright-eyed alertness and numbing fatalism. They can be as nimble as mountain goats or move as sluggishly as prisoners chained together, dragging their feet. They are humorous and quick to giggle over nothing; at the same time they seem to be affected by a profound sadness which marks their faces, their art, their entire civilization.

One concludes that they would be so much better off if left totally alone in their mountains, where they seem quite capable of resurrecting their civilization, even another empire. The presence of strangers seems to confound them utterly. Just as the illiterate, illegitimate Francisco Pizarro and his gang of murdering pig farmers were able to bring down a mighty nation, today's pressures and intruders continue to prevent the Indian from realizing his destiny.

No question that as a people they are possessed of a unique genius. Their survival in today's world seems a miracle. They are like animals who refuse to build nests or go to their lairs while enemies are nearby.

Their industriousness, endurance, and ability to labor under the most severe conditions never fail to impress. Yet, it is as if, ever since Pizarro first set foot on their shore, they've been paralyzed, unable to move one way or another. And yet, since that time when they first met the European, they go on living at altitudes where no one else can breathe, and probably have changed their ways as little as any race on the planet. They obstinately carry on exactly as before. It may be a clever game they are collectively playing. A waiting game—waiting for the white man to go away.

*December 17, Cerro de Pasco—4,438 meters (14,557 feet) above sea level. Cerro de Pasco Guest House $5.00.*

Yow! Talk about a wind that "cuts like a butcher's knife!" (Tennessee Williams). This frigid gale howling down from the hills slices through my poncho, goes right for the ribs.

The streets are lined with coal shops. A siren shrieks, and Indian miners stream out of the ground. An arctic sun sets over their shacks. Sores, I am told, do not heal easily in this cold. Oxygen-starved, the fire in my bedroom just glows, no matter how much I encourage it with the bellows. It doesn't give out much heat.

Bus fare Huanuco-Cerro de Pasco: $1.50.

The bus driver's mottoes, as pasted on the windshield:

SOY SOLTERO
LA CASADA ES MI MUJER*

EL MATRIMONIO ES
LA UNICA GUERRA
DONDE LOS ENEMIGOS
DUERMEN JUNTOS**

Indian eyes: eternally apprehensive . . . as from centuries of trotting along high sierra trails, looking nervously upwards with furrowed worried brow at looming soggy cliffs, precarious rock formations and overladen snowfields, poised to plunge downwards.

Diminutive hatted women, with long skirts and great bundles, trot along, leading or carrying children with bright chapped cheeks.

Andean seagulls . . . llamas drift through snowfields among millstones dating from the time of the Spanish colonial era. God, these mining towns can be grim. The head aches, the heart beats in an unfamiliar manner. Could it be a case of *siroche,* or mountain sickness? Otherwise, I am quite content to bundle up against the biting wind off the naked altiplano.

After weeks in the tropics, I needed this. I want to be in the sierra now. That sharp sunlight I felt warm on my back this morning as I crossed a swinging a suspension bridge to visit ruins 1,000 years old. The clarity of air and vistas. Feeling myself more sharply defined—good!

* I'm single | The married one is my wife
** Marriage is | The only war | Where the enemies | Sleep together

*Decvember 18*

Up at 5 AM to catch the train to Lima.

Menacing chain-link fences topped with barbed wire, arc lamps that shine all night, and sentry boxes give this Cerro de Pasco Corporation compound the appearance of a concentration camp. A miners' strike, which was to have begun this morning, has been postponed 24 hours, so it looks as if I'll be able to get down the mountain.

Warning: stay away from alcohol at these high altitudes, as it brings on ferocious headaches against which aspirin is no avail. Best remedy is to drink water, lots of it.

*9 AM. In the Andes*

Yikes, it's cold up here! Glad I've got my poncho which, like the loose-fitting Moroccan *djellaba,* sensibly insulates one in an envelope of body-heated air. This has to be one of the coldest railroad rides in the world—not at all like the one I remember from my first visit to Peru and wrote about in *The Attempt.* First class used to be spacious and warm, with excellent service and hot food. But the price of a ticket has remained so low ($2.50) that the most impoverished *serrano* can now apparently afford first class for himself and his family. So here we are, all squeezed in together. No heating and the man across the aisle is dying. His son nevertheless spoons breakfast down the unwilling throat, and it all comes back as a mess on the table.

We were rattling along, when all of a sudden the train left the tracks and hurtled into a pasture, with a bunch of scared llamas running around. Chaos. Hundreds of Indians jumped down. I realized I was the only white man among them.

Out of nowhere, a bus came bumping along. I threw my baggage aboard and we rumbled merrily down toward the capital.

In Latin America, the hard hat carries much status. The man who owns one wears it everywhere, not just on the job. The message is that the man works, not just at some menial chore, but at a job he's proud of, in the employ of some stable company that pays well, looks out for its men, and cares for their safety. One sees them of many different colors.

*Hotel Bolivar, Lima.* Expensive, but after a series of Amazonian flea-bags I needed a bit of luxury and comfort.

*Memories of Lima:*

Dating from my first jaunt with college friends through South America in 1958, and from the more prolonged and focused adventures with Joe McPhillips, in 1959, '60-'61 and '64, I began to keep this diary, and, at his insistence, to read and therefore to think seriously about writing for the first time in my life. During the long walks and the long talks, when we ate and enjoyed the Peruvian food and drink (mainly pisco), we felt not only at home but an affection bordering on passion for the streets of Lima. We travelled by bus, truck and train over the Andes, and by balsa raft and steamboat *(vapor)* down the waterways of the upper Amazon. It was here in Peru, I realize now, that I learned the meaning of my youth and my freedom, and felt the powerful creative forces contained within.

Yes, and dating from those days which were perhaps freer than any others, I have always relished an encounter with Hispanic culture. From Tangier I often cross the Strait of Gibraltar to Spain, for flamenco and to sample the *mariscos, tapas,* the tiny coffees and the rough brandies of Andalucia.

And now I'm back in South America, for the first time on my own, imbibing the lonely atmosphere of the Indian bars, where the language-spirit of drinking and talking is Spanish, the language of adventure which I have always associated with my original taste of freedom. The sound of it still propels me to put down on paper what these places do to me . . .

*11 PM*

After seeing *Clockwork Orange* in Spanish, I walked the dark streets of this city I once knew quite well, now hardly at all, although many landmarks are familiar. I wonder where I'm going, that is, what it is that I have to say? Probably I'm saying it right now.

To date this trip has not been easy or especially enjoyable. It's been hard going for a number of reasons, and I foresee leaner times ahead. But that, after all, was the original purpose of the voyage, aside from completing the book—to seek the tough and lonely road and to learn from it what one can. Seeing that movie only reconfirmed my burning need for expression, but who knows if any of what I put down here is profound or just trite. Probably somewhere in between. It's all in the effort, I suppose.

Plaza San Martín and the Plaza de Armas bear restrictions against cars and therefore have retained a degree of the peace and openness that I remember. No more do the neon dice roll down, casting lots over the sleeping figures in the park. The trams no longer rattle down to Callao or anywhere, anymore. I had thought that the mighty Coca Cola sign on Avenida Wilson, lavish symbol of gringo power, would have been pulled down by now, but there it is, still flashing away as it did back in 1960. A host of modern concrete buildings has usurped the park along Avenida Wilson, where a row of slender royal palms once stood like a file of stately soldiers. Many more whores in evidence . . . male and female . . . more brazen than ever. On the whole the center of the city seems more orderly and prosperous. The affluent suburbs I imagine have changed little, but the *barriadas* or shanty towns have definitely mushroomed. I notice new little corner cement parks—an idea that probably filtered down from Manhattan.

When one sees, smells, and is obliged to rub shoulders with masses of fellow human beings, in this case the Peruvians, one feels mingled pity, consanguinity, disgust and indifference, predominantly the latter. When one is confronted with one's brothers in their teeming, squalid and impoverished numbers, the first instinct is to get away from them, to carve some space for one's own life, the few years that remain of it, before the planet is simply overwhelmed by people deprived of every impulse but the struggle, like the myriad plants in the steaming jungle, groping for light and life.

Where is order, except in passivity and fear? Where is form if not supplied by the military? Where direction besides spread and multiplication? Where beauty except where man's hand has not yet touched? Confronted by hordes of strangers, I don't seem to know anything, I lose my way, and this makes me weary.

*December 19*

A letter from Peggy Hubrecht in Amsterdam, thanking me for letting Madeleine come to Holland to help her care for Daan. Daan and Peggy lived on the Old Mountain, the most romantic and mysterious road in Tangier. It wound uphill through palm and pine past shadowy villas half concealed in overgrown gardens. A rustic crowd frequented this road—fishermen, wood choppers, chanting women bent over beneath bundles of sticks bound for the bread ovens, donkeys loaded with firewood for the hammans, girls balancing bunches of flowers on their heads, and goatherds leading their animals. Massive eucalyptus trees let down a flickering light. Occasionally you caught a glimpse of the sea.

Daan was Dutch. Tall, serene and very good-looking, he had led an adventurous life in the East Indies. But his demeanor was tinged by sadness, for he had lost his only son by a previous marriage in a helicopter accident. Peggy was English. Her loud and friendly nature masked the insecurity of being married to such a handsome man. Her restless social energy ensured they led a hectic party life. On my stroll down from where I once lived near the top of the Old Mountain I sometimes dropped by for a drink.

One winter evening I walked in and was introduced to an attractive Dutch woman, a niece of Daan. She was visiting Tangier with her one-year-old daughter, on her way to join her husband who was a vet in Kenya. Her gray-green eyes, erect posture, long auburn hair and stylish clothes created a stir in Tangier. Some people were fascinated by her aristocratic beauty; others were put off by her haughty manner. She spoke fluent English and French. She had lived for several years in Swaziland and South Africa, and her views on life reflected that experience. Her main interest was animals, especially wild animals.

I invited her to the circus, one of the wandering, down-at-the-heel European circuses that occasionally wintered in Morocco. We inspected the undernourished animals in their cages. During the wild animal act we were sitting in the front row, just outside the bars. The Spanish lion tamer cracked his whip. A scrawny male lion jumped onto his perch, turned around and squirted me with a thick stream of hot urine. Madeleine nearly fell out of her chair laughing. I was trying to wipe the stuff off with a handkerchief. After helping me clean up she rested her head on my shoulder.

Later we kissed. That she was married with a small child didn't seem to be an impediment. Maybe the smell of lion turned her on.

It might not have gone farther than that, when an incident occurred that bound us together.

I was riding the bus, one of the new sky-blue Volvos imported by the R.A.T.T. *(Regie Anonyme des Transposts Tangerois)* to replace the aging fleet of brown and yellow Renaults.

Like a block of ice hewn from a Scandinavian glacier, the bus was inching its way through Dradeb, one of the city's poorest barrios, known to foreign residents as "Suicide City" because so many accidents happened there. It was market day, and the bus was pushing ahead of it a moraine of Moroccans intent on getting their shopping done before the day stoked up.

Near the bottom of the Old Mountain where the street crossed Jew's River—a parched gully most of the year, a dangerous and destructive torrent during the rainy season—the bus lurched to a stop. The passengers crowded to the windows on one side, causing the bus to list. An accident had occurred. Trailing the black tail of a skid mark, a motorbike lay on the pavement. A boy with a bloody arm was sitting beside it. Jammed up against the curb near the corner of the bridge was a blue Volkswagen beetle with a Gibraltar license plate. It looked as though the car had swerved to avoid the oncoming motorbike which nevertheless had crashed straight into it.

I recognized the VW right away. It belonged to the Hubrechts. Looking down from the bus window directly above the car, I couldn't see the driver, only a pair of hands gripping the wheel. The Moroccans were pressing so densely about the car that she couldn't open the door.

Jumping down from the bus, I pushed my way through the

crowd and tapped on the window. The tense, frightened expression on her face transformed instantly into one of relief. I went to the boy and saw that he was not seriously hurt. I rode a motorcycle in those days and showed him that his machine was not badly damaged. We took him to a local dispensary where a Moroccan nurse bandaged his arm. For rescuing her from the hooded Moors Madeleine thanked me with hugs and kisses. After that we were together every day.

So. I have had my shoes shined by *LOS INTOCABLES DEL ESPEJO (LUSTRA DEL ESPEJO-5 SOLES)*.* I have had myself photographed in Plaza San Martín. Note the gleaming shoes. I passed a café—El Bambu Tea Room—the sight of which stopped me in my tracks as memory clicked in, beckoned me to retrace my steps and stick my nose through the door. Upon a second look I understood that this café was where Joe McPhillips and I had an intense conversation back in 1960 or '61. What we talked about I cannot recall, but the excitement we both felt in one of those booths lived in me again. In that particular conversation and in countless others like it we charted a course of action, framed by a vaguely conceived quest for an earthly paradise. When the coffee idea didn't work out, the trail led from Peru to Italy through Africa, to France and finally back to Africa. Morocco.

Last spring, I think it was, I told Joe I thought I was in need of a period of determined and prolonged solitude to lift my writing. I was fed up with my sedentary life in Marrakesh. What I ought to do was to say *hasta la vista* to the people I cared about, exit Morocco, and spend the next year or so on the road, moving from one town or country to the next, living in hotels and out of suitcases, and leave all cares behind, except

*The masters of the mirror (Mirror Shine-5 *soles)*.

those of the writer. This drastic step would be required if I were ever to get to the bottom of the problem of myself as a writer. Knowing that my writing is fuelled by solitude, movement and the asceticism they imply, I felt I ought to experience them as intensely as possible and see what happens.

Which is precisely what I'm doing now. Trouble is, I am desperately lonely and miss all my friends. I've seen enough hotel rooms. I want my mud house in the Marrakesh oasis back, plus my old routine. I am often bored—and not at all sure what I'm doing here, or what it is I'm supposed to be looking for, or how any of this will contribute to future works. THE GRIM SOLITUDE IS UPON ME, which is what I presumably longed for, so now I must face it, but the prospects of the encounter seem bleak indeed. I mean, why must everything take so long? Is anything happening? Am I really learning anything new about myself? Nothing memorable has occurred so far, or at least I don't think it has. No new and elucidating personalities have crossed my path. A lot of territory has been covered, most of it not particularly new, and much of it trotted over rather impatiently, with my eyes fixed on the ever-receding horizon. Half the time bored, half the time lonely. What to do with these movements? Haven't I seen enough statued plazas and teeming markets? Not already explored the dusty slums of a half-dozen sweating capitals? Viewed enough jungle and river and mountain to slake my thirst for wilderness? What more have they to teach me? What the hell is it I'm after? I hear a voice whisper . . . illusion and escape. Yes, but there must be a further lesson to be gained from being back here in this "cradle of my learning." I must endure the recurring loneliness and despair and boredom and indecision. WHY AM I NOT REJOICING over the luxury of freedom, movement, new vistas ahead, and all the possibilities contained within? Jesus, does any of this make any sense?

Once more I have been welcomed into the heart of the Benavides family. Joe and I were first introduced to Ismael Benavides back in 1960 by John Paton Davies. Davies was the distinguished American diplomat who, having been railroaded out of the Foreign Service, found a refuge for himself and his large (seven children) family in Lima, which his wife Patricia dubbed their "fur-lined foxhole."

Ismael Benavides is a man of such civility. Last night I felt for him again the same welling up of tenderness and affection. These feelings recalled to me our visit to his beautiful farm in the mountains. I still hear, with an intensity that time cannot erase, the midnight peacock screech and the rumble of a distant landslide up in the Andes.

Ismael was then a stocky gentle man in his mid-forties. Bald, with a round face, bushy eyebrows and soft, deep-set eyes, he had a shy smile and serene manner. A farmer and family man, he exuded warmth and sensitivity. His children were continually running up and throwing their arms around him. He had studied agriculture at Louisiana State University. Mrs. Benavides had been raised in England. All their children had been to English schools in Lima. The whole family spoke fluent English.

Ismael likes to joke that the prefix "Ben" in front of his name means that his family might have descended from Jewish or Arab stock back in Spain. I point out that in Tangier the arabized version of the same name is Benabid. It tickles him to think he might have distant relatives in Morocco.

Unlike many of the old established families in Peru, the Benavides have never been the absentee landlords of various farms and ranches scattered around the country; nor are they the owners of mines. The family has traditionally served the state, and over the years has provided it with some distinguished diplomats and ministers. Ismael's uncle Oscar R. Benavides was president of the Republic back in the 1930's.

The Benavides' principal asset was Huamani farm, which had been in the family since the time of the Conquest. It was located near Ica, about a three-hour ride south of Lima. Back in 1960 Ismael drove Joe and me down there for a visit.

As I recall now, and described in *The Attempt,* the farm nestled in a sloping narrow valley between two spurs of arid mountains. The land was cultivated right up to the rock escarpments on either side. A pair of enormous pines towered above lesser trees, among which the white walls of the hacienda reflected the afternoon sun. The twin pines had been planted centuries ago, when men wore armor, to mark the farm for visitors travelling on horseback across the coastal desert. In the midst of so much desolation, it was like arriving at an oasis.

Ismael proudly showed us around the place he loved so much. Cotton used to be the main crop, but the farm produced hardly enough food to feed the Indians who worked it.

"You need slave labor to make a cash crop out of cotton these days," he told us. "Unfortunately, a lot of farms in Peru are still being run that way."

He ploughed up the cotton and planted avocados and apple trees, importing a special variety of apple from Australia, called Tropical Beauties, that did well in a dry climate. While the trees were maturing he cultivated vegetables and raised chickens to ensure that everyone on the farm had enough to eat. With their own hands Ismael and the Indians built a dam up in the mountains to trap an adequate supply of water to irrigate the crops when the river ran dry, which it did each summer. A miniature hydroelectric plant was installed to bring electricity to the farm. He planted vines and began to produce his own pisco, bottled with a distinctive Huamani label of his own design.

Then, a year or so ago, there was a *golpe,* or coup d'etat in

Lima. A left-wing military junta led by General Juan Velasco Alvarado seized power and threw out the democratically elected government of Fernando Belaunde Terry. Belaunde was a close friend of Ismael and had offered him the post of Minister of Agriculture in his government, but Ismael turned him down because he wanted to devote his energies to Huamani.

General Velasco proclaimed a radical program of land reform, and one of the first farms to be expropriated was Huamani. On Oct 3rd this year truckloads of city Indians arrived to occupy the place. They ate the chickens and stripped the trees of fruit before it was ripe, finally cutting down the trees for firewood. The farm that Ismael had worked so hard to improve, not just for himself and his family but also for the Indians who lived there, quickly subsided into ruin.

I wonder now—Huamani wasn't a big farm as farms in Peru go, a thousand acres more or less, but was one of the first to be confiscated. Was that because Ismael had been a friend of the deposed president, Belaunde?

Although Ismael has stoically accepted his fate, I think the loss of Huamani must have broken his heart. He had worked the farm all his life. His children had spent their holidays there. He had been attached to the place heart and soul. Now he had nowhere to go. He is a farmer without a farm.

*December 21*
*Rest. Chalaquito, Callao*

Callao at sunset, where ships waiting to enter the harbor float like logs on the orange sea.

Fat tough whores plucking at my sleeve: "Fucky fucky? Téléfon?" (their word for 69).

In the restaurant:

CONSULT YOUR POCKET BEFORE EATING
PAY FOR THE FIRST TO BE SERVED THE SECOND

Lowering clouds cap the dusty brown hills that blockade Lima to the east. The clouds truncate the hills but do not let in the sun. The eye has a choice of dull gray or dull brown—colors that do not excite the spirit. The colors of bad weather, resignation, pollution, cement, the military, drought, dishwater and mouldering excrement. And up, up those barren flanks creep the shanties of misery, the *barriadas.* Indians stumble in from the sierra, spitting their tubercular lungs onto the pavement. Good Lord, with what vain hopes do the mountain folk desert the Andean heights to come down here? No, what *misery* drives them to relinquish their ancestral homes?

The *garua,* the persistent drizzling mist created by the cold Humboldt Current flowing up the Pacific coast from Antarctica, shrouds Lima half the year and is compounded by the emissions of thousands of polluting engines. Last time I was here it triggered an asthma attack which landed me in the hospital. Now I feel my lungs beginning to tighten up again. I am going to have to quit this city soon for the mountains or the coast to find the summer sunshine which should have burnt off this dank weather by now.

These pages, what strength they begin to have! An idea for a short story is rattling around inside my head, but I cannot bring myself to commit more than a few notes to paper. The nagging reluctance to sit down to a new project as I grow weary of hotel rooms, patrolling the streets alone, eating by myself, having no one to talk to. This trip, which began embroidered with so many romantic expectations, is beginning to wear thin. Loneliness and boredom creep in, like mice, to gnaw at the idea of enterprise. Forcing energy and imagination to the surface is like pumping mud through a sieve.

Christmas spirit. Fights constantly break out among the ambulatory vendors who choke Jirón de la Unión and the other main shopping streets, as they jostle for space at the most lucrative positions. The newspapers are full of it, but nothing can be done. The police arrive by the truckload, sirens screaming. They knock a few heads and scatter the mob; but, as soon as they depart, back come the vendors, surging and struggling for the best positions before the brightly lit shops. The officials are confounded. There are just too many *ambulantes* to contend with, surging down from the *barriadas* with their cheap goods.

*December 22*

The way I see it, this military junta is incapable of running Peru with its huge and mainly alienated Andean Indian population. The situation has deteriorated to a point where sooner or later it will probably trigger the emergence of an ultra-radical revolutionary leader who will just shoot everybody on sight. Lima is slowly being throttled by its slums. The capital, in my opinion, should be moved back to Cuzco, ancient heart of the Inca empire, sending the message out that this is Indian country, not Spanish. Lima can remain the commercial capital, like Casablanca in Morocco, but the spiritual and cultural center should be up high, where it belongs, in the Andes, where only the Indians can breathe.

Rosalinda told me about her home. (We met at the Benavides' Christmas party and sipped coffee afterwards in a bar off Colmena.) Her two brothers are crippled with muscular dystrophy, and her sister in the States has made it known that her young son is showing the first disturbing signs of the disease.

(As babies Rosalinda's two stricken brothers walked on tiptoes. When the doctor examined them, he explained to the father, who had been exhorting his sons to walk flat-footed, that his method was incorrect. Neither boy ever walked again.)

Rosalinda is worried that she too might be a carrier of the disease and could transmit it to her child, should she have one. Women carry the disease, but only males in the family come down with it. The whole household is plagued by the disease and the resulting guilt.

Rosalinda cut short her stay in Paris because she felt her brothers needed her. While she was away, her grandfather died. As she never saw him dead, for her he lives still, and she resents her father for sitting in her grandfather's chair, and her sister, when she visited, for sleeping in his bedroom.

After she came home, the garden sprinkler broke. She got it working and compulsively set out to fix everything that had been neglected. She mended clothes, looked in drawers for buttons, wrote letters, cleaned out the fridge, and put the whole house in order.

Her grandfather—for her he was her father, because he was around the house all day, while her own father usually returned from work after she had gone to bed—was extremely meticulous. In his world, every object had its *sitio.*

They used to go sailing together. And although her grandfather rarely spoke, except to issue a sailing order—"Pull this." "Tie that rope there," etc.—it had been a complete, if silent experience for the girl. She and her grandfather had known each other well. She pleased him. They didn't have to talk much.

Now, at 30, Rosalinda thinks about the joy of producing a baby. She has fallen in love, which changed her life. She will go to New York for a series of complicated tests which will determine whether she is a carrier of the disease or not. Her brothers, meanwhile, although confined to wheelchairs, are becoming more and more difficult as the disease advances.

They refuse the special diet. "While I still live, I want to eat what pleases me, damn it!" Both are educated, one a lawyer.

And Rosalinda—dark, intelligent, morbidly introspective, nervous and calm, looking no more than eighteen—prepares herself for a flight from home.

"In order to fly, the wings must be exercised. Passion produces passion. Need produces need. They don't need me as much as I thought they did. It's me who needs to be needed. I want to have a baby one day. I want to move out."

She looked right at me when she said this.

But will she ever?

*December 23*

What interests me now is logic—the logic of events building to an inevitable conclusion. The logic of character leading inexorably to its unavoidable fate . . . the rude logic that landscape and other forces will impose on the working out of the tale. This logic may not at first be evident but the reader, having finished the book and reflecting upon the succession of pages, will conclude there was only one possible outcome. Yes, a book in which all forces combine to provide thrust toward a destiny which has been locked up from the very first page.

*December 24, 10 AM*

Stunned by the news on the radio that an earthquake has devastated Nicaragua. Managua is down, a city in ruins. The Gran Hotel, where we stayed almost exactly two months ago, a pile of rubble. So the birds resting in the façade of the *teatro* knew something all along. They knew something bad was coming. They were ready to move out at a moment's notice.

Today Sra. Ferreyros, cousin of the Ismael Benavides family, invited me to a picnic with her husband and children on the beach south of Lima.

The tide was out, the beach looked half-a-mile wide, nobody on it, with the big Pacific surf pounding in the distance. Blazing sun and sand so hot you could hardly walk on it. Rosita (Sra. Ferreyros) unpacked the picnic and went off for a swim by herself. I was sitting under the umbrella with Sr. Ferreyros and the children when I noticed her waving at us from the ocean. We all saw her, far away because the beach was so wide, and we all waved back. Nobody paid much attention because we were all hungry and tucking into the lunch she had prepared; but to me there was something odd about the way she waved, like she was trying to tell us something. Still chewing on a piece of fried chicken, I got up and meandered down toward the water. Pretty soon I broke into a run because the sand was scorching my feet. Maybe it was that run that saved her, because if I had arrived a minute later, it might have been too late.

The closer I got to the water, the more certain I became that something was wrong. The mountainous Pacific breakers were rolling over her. She kept disappearing under the water, resurfacing, and waving. Then another comber buried her. It wasn't the happy wave of a woman enjoying herself in the ocean, but a frantic signal of distress.

The minute I entered the surf, I understood what the problem was. A powerful river of cold water was pulling at my legs. Memories of Mazatlán. I was only standing knee-deep, but it was all I could do to keep my balance. I waded out through the waves, up to my shoulders, until I was able to grab hold of her hand. It was a long struggle to get her back to the beach. She was exhausted from fighting the current.

Nevertheless, she had a drowning man's arm-lock around my neck that nearly choked me. For a minute I thought we'd both had it. The waves kept crushing us. They rolled us so deep I thought we'd never get back to the air again. Finally, we staggered onto the sand. For several minutes she lay in the shallow water. Like people shipwrecked we rested and slowly got our wits back.

I led her back to her family, but no one said anything. Maybe Sra. Ferreyros was too worn out to talk. A life-and-death drama had taken place right in front of her family, but she didn't mention it. It was strange. I don't think the children had any idea their mother was in difficulty. Sr. Ferreyros was taking a nap.

Christmas Eve. What they call religion in my own country leaves me indifferent, but here in Lima I willingly go down on my knees with the Indian multitude on the cold stone floor of the cathedral.

*Christmas Day, 1972*

A Christmas cable from Madeleine, far away in Holland. She signed with the words *sabes todo,* our codeword for love but she did not say who she is spending Christmas with or how to communicate. I hesitate sending a letter to her home address, where it might be intercepted, torn up, and thrown away.

Christmas lunch alone in Raimondi's restaurant. Ceviche could be the complete diet: raw fish *(corvina)* marinated in lime juice, raw onion and fresh coriander, accompanied by a cold sweet potato and a chunk of cold corn on the cob (*choclo*) to absorb the heat of the chili (*aji*).

Solitude chosen has nothing to do with solitude circumstance.

What was Ezra Pound's quote? Test your sincerity through the development of style?

From now on a worthwhile concern could be to examine myself and learn what I'm really writing about.

The elevator goes up and the elevator goes down. For most it's a means of avoiding the stairs; for Jane Bowles it's a source of recurring claustrophobia.

"I love space more than you."
"Yes, but I fear enclosure less."

New Year's resolution: not to exaggerate.

Good bookshops here, where I can renew my supply of reading material. Now into Carlos Castaneda's *Journey to Ixtlán*. In all three of his books, whether they're fact or fiction, it is evident to me that the author is susceptible to hypnotism, which Don Juan instantly understood when he shot him that piercing look in the Arizona bus station. (cf. The wedding guest in Coleridge's *The Rhyme of the Ancient Mariner*.) He perceived the effect one glance had on the young man. He had a hypnotic hold over Castaneda from the beginning.

Don Juan's words ring disturbingly clear, especially down here. They touch at the edge of my own thought. He encourages expansion and commitment, responsibility and mobility —the mobility of the hunter, who lightly touches all things, never leaving a mark, before moving on.

And this journey upon which I am currently embarked . . . I, too, touch lightly, or not at all, and move on . . . the elusive seeker. My only tracks are to be found here, on this page, which I cover with words.

Strange all this, on the day I have begun yoga exercises, the very day I am able to see with my eyes shut, peering into night skies, clouded and crowded with numberless points of light.

Lying on the floor in the shadowed silence of this hotel room, bathed by the crepuscular glow of sunset over the Pacific, soothed by the peace and uncertainty of this hour, I began to focus the silence of my attention. At first, I was able to assemble before my closed eyes a number of glowing points. The points condense into an incandescent haloed mass. Upon further directing the silence of my attention, I shrank them down to one intensely radiant dot. I found it utterly satisfying to summon them from the vastness of space and to concentrate them in this manner. Through the manipulation of some muscle located behind my eyeballs, I was able to alter the quality of darkness.

*December 26*

The Bolivar is the best hotel I've stayed in so far, maybe ever. Its friendly atmosphere and service are outstanding. When Joe and I came to Lima the first time, we couldn't afford to stay here, but we used every facility the hotel had to offer—phone, cable, restaurant, bar, men's room, etc. We never received complaints, only service, when we turned up ragged and unwashed from another marathon trip into the jungle or over the Andes. We hung around the front desk, reading our mail or writing letters on hotel stationery. Everybody was pleasant and helpful, from the hotel manager down to the elevator boy, and they still are.

He hangs around the entrance to the hotel and Jirón de la Unión. Short, he comes up to my shoulder. Dressed in the non-descript baggy brown suit city Indians seem to favor, he approached me late at night as I returned from a film, and in the morning as I headed out for a cup of coffee on the crowded Unión. As I made my way along, I noticed him by my arm, hurrying to keep up.

"How are you, meester? Do you like Lima? Are you having a good time?"

Then he flashed the gold ring.

As all this had happened before, I thought his eyesight must be defective. Then I realized that he never looks up into the face of the person he's trying to hustle.

But today, when I replied, once again, "No, hombre, no! I don't want your ring," he recognized my voice, looked up and laughed. Giving me an amiable pat on the back, he scurried off, vanishing instantly into the teeming mob.

Rule for the future: following the completion of a work, in my case, *Tangier Buzzless Flies*, take a trip. Go somewhere. Do something different. Make sure you move somewhere, especially if you haven't done so inside your head.

"Shut your eyes. What do you see?"
"Nothing."
"Open them. Now what do you see?"
"The same as before."
"That's what it's like."
"What?"
"Death. You black out, but the world doesn't change."
"That's what you think."
"What do you think?"
"I don't know, but what you say scares the shit out of me."

*December 27/8, midnight*
*Chala, Hotel Turistas $20.50.*

Came here from Lima by collectivo taxi: $8.50. Me and 44

kilos of luggage.

Lunch. Bathed in the post-fish and white-wine glow of sleepy well-being, I forsook a nap and stumbled along the deserted coast for a swim, avoiding the caved-in carcass of a horse that had fallen over the cliff.

Once more I opened my heart to the thundering Pacific. The great green seas scouring the crusty cliffs make me think of the poem *November Surf* by Robinson Jeffers. I stripped and threw myself into the foam. The pounding mountainous waves stuffed my ears with brine and buffeted me without mercy; the roaring water made me temporarily hard of hearing. Reflex waves rebounding off the cliff faces slapped against the incoming swells. Seagulls hovered, pelicans floated and plummeted, cormorants dove for fish beneath the surface. Sea wrack and spindrift—enough to renew one's faith in the purifying power of the planet forever.

I swim with the seals here. Body burning from the frigid sea, I tried jogging along the steep beach but slipped on the greasy tangle of kelp ripped from their moorings and hurled on the sand by these colossal combers.

Restlessly the lion heads thrashed their tails in the deep swell of the Pacific. Pink starfish by the million. Shark heads among the rocks. The bony feathered remains of thousands of pelicans. Sometimes they just die off like flies. Nobody knows why. Dung-whitened sea rocks. Orange crabs scuttled to their holes in the sand, where they waited provocatively. A vulture tugging on a shark's intestine—raw-headed vultures stripping a dead seal—they do their work quickly.

Soaking wet I dressed, left the coast and walked inland.

When I have scaled yet another dusty brown hill, and look back upon the ridge where I stood, perhaps fifteen or twenty minutes earlier, I seem to remember another person, another me, who previously existed upon that flaking ridge, but not the same person who has attained yet another disappointing summit. A man climbs the first hill and stops to gaze back at the view he has made for himself. Looking up, he ascends the next higher, steeper hill, but this will not be the same man.

One particular hill drew my attention. Two pointed rock formations, like a pair of nascent horns, capped its summit. The gap between looked like a vantage point from which I could have a panorama of the desert plain and wild Pacific coast. Standing at the base of this hill, I resolved to make it my final destination for the day.

The ascent was more difficult than I had anticipated. At last I reached the gap between the horns. Instead of taking in the view, as had been my original intention, my attention was arrested by the presence of thousands of miniature cacti which grew there. These cacti had recently put out blue flowers, and the whole of the sandy bowl between the two rock faces was carpeted with them—a velvety blue carpet. Taking a seat among the cacti but not on them, I realized that the depression sheltered them from the wind which blows mercilessly about these stony heights. Examining the flowers closely, thinking to add them to the cactus collection I had recently planted in my garden in the Marrakesh oasis, I picked several and their attendant seed pods, also of a deep blue color. This home of theirs was a quiet place, and I lingered longer than I had intended. The Peruvian coast being a total desert, nothing else grew for miles around.

Later, while making my descent from that summit, I took care to cup the flowers and pods lightly in my hands, lest I bruise them. It was not particularly surprising, therefore, when the seed pods began to fall from my hands onto the ground from which I had taken them. I picked them up again, continued on my way, and thought no more about it. At length I reached the flat, where the going was easier. Although I was able to devote more attention to the flowers and their seeds, they continued to fall from my hands. There seemed nothing I could do to hang onto them. As I bent down to retrieve one, another would fall. Night was also falling, and I had several miles to go back to the hotel.

At last it became clear to me that the cactus flowers were resisting being taken from their cup of earth. The seeds within their pods may have sensed that I was a stranger who would transport them to an alien desert on another continent. Finally I acceded to their mute wisdom. So I let the flowers and the seeds fall where they would and continued on.

Later, I regretted not returning them to their cradle between the two protective rock horns, but night was coming on, and I was afraid of losing my way among those bare brown hills, each indistinguishable from the next, all with the texture of threadbare rugs.

*December 29, Arequipa—the white city, the city of lawyers.*
*Hotel Turistas. $33.15*

And we passed many stupendous accidents along the coastal highway coming up here, so full of drama. A bus that had missed a turn and landed in a deep ravine from which, I was informed, not a single passenger emerged. A truck that had demolished itself against the side of a cliff. An automobile that had been driven blithely off into space, hurtling into the sea 400 feet below. My fellow passengers reverently crossed themselves and mumbled solemn prayers as we thundered past each roadside crucifix.

Name of trucks:

Gray dunes of crescent perfection stud the orange plain like a flock of Arab tents. Volcanic sand had gathered like snow drifts forming a crisp ridge from which the afternoon shadow fell like a knife blade. Sand drifts and snow dunes. The fine dust came in, and I could taste the pumice between my teeth. The bus stops: Indian women camped by the road raised their timid voices like sleepy birds as they held up their goods for sale.

Let's face it, these Indians have been created to survive. Their ancestors migrated here all the way from Asia. Sierra-bound, away from the floods and the bombs, they might well outlast us all.

And from down on the dusty plain, I caught a first glimpse, through the haze of heat and distance, of the great brooding snow-capped volcano that created this landscape—El Misti. It's high here, high and cold. I wrap my poncho around and take deep breaths. The thin, pure Andean air agrees with my lungs.

*December 30/31*

Exiting from yet another cinema at midnight (all South American film showings seem to end at midnight—this one, *Cabaret,* made me almost nostalgic for the sinister insanity of Nazi-infected 1930's Germany), I wobbled through a passage of temporary dislocation, along another dark stone street. Where am I now—Panama? Iquitos? Belén? Paramaribo? Manaus? Tonight, after a moment's bewilderment as the impact of the film wore off, I remembered—it's Arequipa—the white city *(sillar* is the name of the white volcanic stone from which the city is constructed), the city of lawyers, professors, imposing Spanish colonial doorways and churches.

I have visited several of them—the churches, that is—in the city and the surrounding villages. I have listened to the litanies, the endless repetitions and the scuffling of sandals on the cold stone floors. I have noted the genuflections, the sparse attendance, the obviously bored priests. It all makes for such a ponderous, slow-moving scene, utterly dependant upon the suffering of stones and souls.

The one exciting exception being the formidable Convent of Santa Catalina, an entire walled-in village right in the city center. The cloistered nuns—it boggles the imagination to think of what has gone on behind those walls for the past four hundred years.

"Strange predictions and happenings, together with great saintliness and the exercise of exalted virtue."

They writhed in ecstasy, fantasizing about Jesus. As for myself, I could with pleasure take up residence in one of these immaculate stone dwellings, where high-class nuns once lived. The line and the weight of the architecture come straight out of 16th-century Spain.

And so, striding across yet another Plaza de Armas (this one reminding me of the one in Salamanca, in Spain, where the philosopher Miguel de Unamuno faced down the fascists during the Spanish Civil War), up another stone street, through another park, to another hotel room, where I now sit, sipping Huamani pisco straight from the bottle, ruminating and scribbling and jabbering (*blablablabeando*) to myself.

Holding up a forkful of *corvina* and molluscs, I looked about the hotel dining room and felt grateful for good health and sanity. But is it enough? Apparently not. *The Quest* is what the next one ought to be called, if there ever is another one. If I ever get around to tackling the typescript stacked on the table in front of me, that is. Hush, you huddled pile of printed paper! Your hour will come! The fact of the matter is ... I'm too lonely to do anything but fill the pages of this diary. While working on a novel I require company in the evening after the work is done . . . friends to relieve the pressure of writing, and here there is nobody.

And I miss I miss I miss—our adobe house in the Marrakesh oasis, the crystalline Saharan air, and the view of the snow-capped Atlas Mountains framed by date palms. Most of all I miss my imperfect love.

Clipclop, clipclop—how many streets have spoken thus to me? Read a Spanish newspaper in the park, consent to have your shoes shined once again, enter this café for a pisco, head to another for ceviche, cross the street for a beer, to another bar for another shot of pisco. Do the yoga exercises, your callisthenics on the floor of the hotel room, work on this notebook, try to make the mind work in creative patterns. Visit the cathedral, sit in the sun to warm up afterwards, meander through the park, strike up a conversation with an eager student in a deserted sunny plaza, think about sleep. Ignore the nagging pain in your knees. Wonder about your lungs, suck down the mountain air. Try to suppress the stubborn suspicion that this trip is taking you nowhere. Count yourself lucky to have good health and the resources to wander out of time. Return to the coffee shop across the street, repress a desire for cigarettes and for women. Ponder retreat, that is, to a monastery. Reflect on the heavy implications of last night's dream. Fend off the encroaching emptiness. Read, work up an appetite by walking, look over the cinema selections in the local paper, devise plans to fill an evening, work on your Spanish, looking up words in the pocket dictionary. Think about the world, the mess in Vietnam, become depressed, turn it off, think about tomorrow and a personal future, not the world's. Try to stay off the booze. Always exploring, trudging the cobbled streets, by night silent and cool, by day thundered and crunched by the myriad wheeled machines. Think of tomorrow, sunrise, fresh light, another departure, a new trip, perhaps leading to new mindscape and soulscape, never to avoid or turn aside from or forget or fail to linger upon the essential question: IS ANYTHING HAPPENING? Meanwhile the Indians, unconscious, sprawled on the grass, drunk on a Sunday afternoon. One thinks and thinks: often one does not know what one is thinking about as thoughts suddenly lock onto themselves when the perplexed individual catches a glimpse of himself reflected in a shop window.

"Who are you, and what are you all about anyway?"

By God, drink the pisco from the bottle in the hotel room which you alone occupy, look out upon trees and light, hear the birds and wind and count yourself lucky. Breathe the clean mountain air, suck it down and know it doesn't get much better than this. As Don Juan prescribes, perform each act with the impeccable knowledge that it may be your last. And give the next book form—big conclusive form.

A prayer in a church for the loved ones far away in New Jersey, Tangier, and Amsterdam. No phone number and no mailing address. Who will she be spending New Year's Eve with?

Shall we celebrate an ancient virtue? Talk, think, move, look out upon the world, enjoy what you behold, but . . .

DON'T TOUCH
SERVE YOURSELF BY NOT TOUCHING
(Sign in restaurant)

# 1973

Thus the New Year entered, which I observed, with a bellyful of pisco, seated on a stone bench in an antique church square, while the bells clanged and reverberated along the stone alleys, through the parched valleys, the abandoned terraces, repository of agricultural secrets unshared for 500 years since the Conquest, when three *Arequipeñas* burst forth from a stone portal I had been admiring, rushed across the grass to hug me and wish me a Happy New Year. The warmth of their bodies! They raced off again, leaving me shivering in the frigid Andean night as the great bells bonged, firecrackers exploded and rockets hissed upwards, sighed out, and expired in the night. Who will she be with tonight?

The charge that despair gives.

In the streets adjacent to the Plaza de Armas, the Indians had set up tables and chairs on the sidewalk, where they offered pisco and lemon and *anticuchos* (chunks of burnt bull's heart on sticks) and boiled potatoes. As I had no particular cause for joy, I watched the Indians with special interest. In their quiet way they celebrated. They were not drunk—this was not their year entering. They were just there, in their numbing fragile silent numbers.

Don't we all . . . all of us . . . somehow . . . have it . . . a numbing lyrical fragile presence?

Once more I experienced a curious sensation of having been liberated from space and time. The luxury of having my shoes shined in a Latin American plaza, where past and future seem to have been emptied from life. Who in fact wishes another year to be deducted from the already dwindling supply? On feast days, one does not think of tomorrows. Mr. Banfield said God gives a man three score and ten years. I'm 34 ½ years old—half of this life is over. Mine.

A vision of men is accumulating around me. See Johnny travel. Watch him watch the Indians. See him being furtively scrutinized by those he observes. See the stones, piled one upon another to form a wall, or laid one beside another to make a street. Those stones worn soft, smooth and shiny by the passage of a million faithful shuffling feet. Faithful to what—another million faithful feet, still shuffling? The fate of stones and souls: when the firecrackers and the rockets and the *rasca pies* have ceased their thundering, you only hear the silence. The nuns inside Santa Catalina did have an answer—if only for themselves—a pristine response from a privileged few. Form must have meant everything. The secret letters, the bathing adventures. Their architecture you want to hug. They knew things. To close out is to shut in. In silence they perfected mysteries.

*January 1, 1973, Puno, Peru*
*(12,648 feet above sea level). Railroad Hotel $8.00*

This has to be one of the most god-awful, coldest, drabbest, most depressing towns I've ever had the misfortune to find myself stuck in. It is raining, it is hailing, it is freezing cold—and to think I have to spend the next 48 hours here waiting for the boat to Bolivia! How can people live at this altitude, where there's barely enough oxygen for the llamas and the sheep?

Luckily, I have found a friendly bar, have already downed a

couple of piscos and rubbery *anticuchos*. This hotel, miracle of miracles, has hot water in its pipes. I have already taken a shower, an unexpected luxury, even though the water was cut off half way through. My room overlooks the train tracks and the freight yard. Beyond, Lake Titicaca—dark and dreary like a northern wintry sea under lowering skies.

The trip up here was just the kind of train ride I like. Slow, deliberate, with many colorful stops along the way. You can't be in a hurry up here. The railroad car comfortable and uncrowded. Food edible. The land clean and barren, with thrilling vistas. At the first stations, Indian boys sell mountain trout. Bright yellow lichens blotch the blue rocks. This is a land of llamas and bowler hats, appropriate to Indian formality. The bleak and blasted mining communities at 13, 14, 15 thousand feet, like the last towns on earth, which one day they probably will be—after the bombs have fallen. Snowfields, a hailstorm, getting colder and colder . . . And they will play soccer at these altitudes, the icy wind whipping dust away from the players' feet. Women in voluminous skirts huddle together in the lea of mud walls, their tiny brown children bundled in ponchos, shawls, layers of sweaters. Seagulls, ducks, and coots gather at the unfrozen waterholes upon the vast greenish tundra. At the shriek of the railroad whistle the birds take flight for the safety of the marshes. Fragile souls—burdened with immortality and fearing metal—they take wing over the gloomy expanse of the tundra and head home to the reed beds.

When an Indian smiles at you, the whole face smiles. Then the smile stops, and the mask of the Andes comes down.

Two distant figures in a landscape, detected by a swift wind movement—the whipped poncho, the lifted scarlet skirt. Where could they be headed, with nothing beyond but the eternal frozen plain? 4,447 *metros sobre el nivel del mar.* Run llama run!

When the train stops, the villagers scramble for newspapers. They're starving—for news. Most can read. Half the population consists of *ambulantes,* who besiege and board the train at each stop, sometimes by the dozen, sometimes by the hundred, selling everything under the sun.

"This bone-strewn land."

Brrr, this solitary travel experience can be grim. How many grade B films in unheated grade B movie houses have I sat through, just to pass the time? How much grade B food and booze have I consumed, just to fill my belly or to staunch a flow of tears? In how many grade B beds in grade B hotels have I laid my head, wishing I were elsewhere? And how many hours of grade B solitude—strictly bored and non-creative—have I passed? Even my dreams have become of such grade B interest that I have ceased to write them down. Noises outside. I went to the window and looked down. People were moving around in the dark. Soldiers searching the neighboring houses. Guns. They were kicking down doors and leading people away. The whole scene was becoming too ominous for words. And these icy rains are just beginning. I better get myself out of these mountains quick. Even more lethal rains are to be expected in the lowlands—the tropical rains which never let up. Thank God they've turned on the central heating. My feet had become so cold and clammy I could hardly believe these dying things belonged to me.

I want sunlight and warmth but most of all I yearn for the company of people who mean something to me. I've seen enough strangers.

The sadness of this Andean music, the *tristes* and *huainitos*

—enough to break your heart. The chants of the Sahara, New Orleans jazz . . . my heart goes out to ethnic music whose soul is pain.

Excellent anise *(najar)* here. It has an apple taste. Potatoes and onions also of the best quality. Fifteen years ago, headed the other way, I was in this town, just twenty years old, with two Princeton friends and a blanket made of vicuña skins I had smuggled out of Bolivia in an airline bag. Now it is draped over the sofa in my mother's living room in Far Hills, NJ. I can hardly recall who I was then. It seems that I have all too successfully blocked out years 1-20. Deliberately erased my "personal history" until I took up the pen on that first trip through South America and began to write it all down.

Yes, Johnny McBride, Don Erdman and I took the train from here to Cuzco, where we spent the night in another railroad hotel. I do remember that night well, for I slept more deeply than any other night in my life. The next morning I was literally thrown out of bed by an earth tremor. Strange I should remember that one particular night, when all I did was sleep. It was that sense of exquisite refreshment, the result of impeccable sleep. It is as though the second phase of my life began there, that morning in the railroad hotel in Cuzco, lying stunned on the floor while the earth shook and the overhead light swung crazily, like a pendulum gone berserk.

Writing is all about integrity and survival, and the struggle to explore the essential nature of sanity.

*January 2. Bar Restaurant El Lago*

The professor slumps at the bar. It is as if he has no spine. Each time he lifts his glass, however, he sits up straight. His back stiffens like that of a marine at attention while he sips his drink.

"Now look here, professor . . ."

"Do not interrupt! I am a student of the absurdity, the comedy of life, and the lyricism contained within. When I have visions, I laugh. Do not speak to me of the hideous waste, the evil!"

He slumps again.

*January 3/4 (midnight)*

Conrad's Kurtz and Lowry's Consul—each unhinged by the power of his vision. Having stepped over the threshold of ordinary reality, having glimpsed the crack, having been made both wise and mad, return to normal life was out of the question. Castaneda, with a teacher to guide him, survived. Had he gone it alone, he'd still be out there, bones gnawed by gila monsters, pushing up sagebrush.

"The buying and selling crowd who run this rotten show."
—Joseph Conrad

Along the shore of Lake Titicaca sit Indian women in black bowler hats and colorful clothes. Wads of coca puff out their cheeks. The sierra sky—dark blue going on black. Condors at 18,000 feet. They can kill a man by rushing down the side of a mountain and knocking him off his burro, then yank out his guts at the bottom of the abyss.

*Midday*

Sitting in the sun on the wharf, waiting for the good ship *Ollanta* to depart across the lake for Bolivia (overnight passage to Guaqui $8.00), I watched the old steam cranes at work. "Donkeys," they're called. Their maker Thomas Smith will be long dead, and his Son, too. The machines must be a hundred years old, but they're still in fine working order. What nostalgia they summon up—dipping and swinging their heads over the quaysides of London and Liverpool when the British Empire was at its height, exporting goods for the world. And the docks of Calcutta, Singapore, Hong Kong—what cargoes they must have swung over the teak-decked ships. Conrad must have known them well.

They say the *Ollanta* was transported by rail in sections from the coast to these mountains and assembled, piece by piece, probably by these cranes, on this shore of Lake Titicaca.

I miss . . . I miss . . . I miss . . . Too often, instead of travelling with a light and open spirit through these wild and exotic lands, with as much time as I need to accomplish my purposes as they arise, I fear my ears are closed to the song emitted by this creaky accordion called freedom. Enduring the empty hotel rooms, the cold beds, the dark streets, the movie houses, the bars and restaurants infested with strangers. Something wrong here—I do not accept my solitude, nor listen to its promise. I have been spoiled by the people who love me. They have spoiled my solitude, by loving me and by not being here with me.

*January 6, La Paz. Hotel Crillon ($71.00)*

Where a letter from M awaited me. The last time we were so far apart we were on opposite sides of Africa. She promised to come back to Tangier, but when she flew away with Julie to join her husband in Kenya, I didn't know if I would ever see her again. The only way to communicate was by mail. I wrote every day, sometimes more than once a day, to a place called Kericho, in Kenya, East Africa.

Back to Tangier she came in the spring, but this time without Julie. It shocked everyone that she had left her daughter behind. Madeleine did not have strong maternal instincts. She had already abandoned her daughter once before. Julie had been born in Swaziland, where Madeleine had relatives. Her mother arrived from Holland to see her new granddaughter. Madeleine promptly handed over her newborn baby to take back to Holland, while she and her husband went on an extended driving tour of South Africa and Namibia. Madeleine told me that her mother joked that when Madeleine returned from Africa to Holland she was going to line up a row of babies and see if Madeleine could recognize her own child.

The Hubrechts had been scared off by Madeleine's parents who accused them of encouraging our relationship. They refused to let her stay in their house. My mother flew from New York to meet her. My mother liked Madeleine but took a dim view of my involvement with the married mother of a small child.

We drove across southern Morocco in my VW convertible and made plans to go to America. Madeleine felt at home in Morocco. She loved Africa and did not want to live in Holland. She enjoyed shopping in the native markets. Love of exotic food and travel were two things we had in common. We both drank and smoked. She was a heavy smoker of French cigarettes—Gauloises and Gitanes.

We visited the mud farmhouse I had rented in the Marrakesh oasis. La Petite Maison, as it was called, was hidden in a mixed orchard of olive, pomegranate, lemon and tangerine trees. I introduced her to the Moroccan family who looked after the place. Caftan, his wife Zohra, his witch-like mother Madame Caftan, and their little children. They weren't sure who Madeleine was, but they welcomed her like a member of the family. They were glad to see a woman with me, because for them it meant stability, that I might stay longer. The house had just three small rooms—kitchen, living room and bedroom. The living conditions were pretty basic: no hot water, no electricity and no telephone. But there were advantages. The place had been furnished by my Russian landlady with French antiques. A continual supply of pure fresh water that flowed underground from the Atlas Mountains was pumped by a green Lister engine from deep within a well. Marrakesh could be as hot as blazes in summer and freezing cold in winter, but the thick adobe walls protected you from the extremes in temperature. A strong-drawing fireplace and kerosene lamps heated the place pretty well. There was absolute peace, and you couldn't beat the timeless beauty of the oasis or the view of the snow-capped High Atlas. You were cut off from the world, as much as you wanted to be. The Grand Sahara beckoned from the other side of the mountains, but if you felt like a dry martini, Abdeslam in the bar of the Mamounia was an expert. Marrakesh with its international airport was just five miles away.

Then Madeleine flew home to Holland to face the music.

A month later I joined her in Amsterdam. We drove around Holland. I learned about raw herring, smoked eel, and sampled the many varieties of cheese and beer. We visited a working windmill. She explained how dikes were made and described the huge storms that knocked them down. It was like a trip back to my childhood when I first learned about this quaint and singular country from my schoolbooks.

Meanwhile, other forces were at work. My hotel room was raided by the police sent by Madeleine's father who had concluded that his daughter's strange behavior must be caused by drugs. We sat on the bed while they searched the room. There was nothing, and they went away empty-handed.

Madeleine's mother agreed to meet us in a roadside café. The Hoogwelgeboren Vrowe Mevrow J.L.A. Clifford Kocq van Breugel—Baronesse van Nagell was an attractive woman in her fifties. She inquired where my family came from in America. Where I had gone to university. What books I had written and what my father did. She was courteously sizing me up. Madeleine had mentioned that her mother thought she had married beneath her. She asked if I were related to Harry Hopkins, President Roosevelt's special wartime assistant, and seemed disappointed when I said I was not. She wanted to know how long I intended to stay in Morocco. When I said I had no plans to leave, I could see she was not pleased by my answer. She did not like the idea of her daughter and especially her granddaughter living in Morocco.

It was arranged for me to meet Madeleine's husband. M drove me to an outdoor café near a canal and instructed me to sit at an unoccupied table under a tree. Then she went away. I sat there feeling nervous and not knowing what to expect—maybe a punch in the nose. A dark-haired man approached. Martin Vermooten had been an officer in the Dutch army. He was a world-class show jumper. He had rugged good looks and looked pretty tough.

He sat down and ordered beers. I soon realized that I had misjudged him. He seemed more bewildered than hostile. More than once he referred to my letters.

"Those letters, those damned letters. Every day one arrived, every day! Those letters were the reason we left Kenya and came back here. I had a job, a home, a wife and a family. Now I don't have any of those things, all because of those letters."

Evidently he had given up on his wife. His main concern was his daughter. He questioned me on how we planned to take care of her in America.

"What do you know about babies?" he asked.

"Not much. But I'm sure we can find a nanny to help us."

"And where are you going to find a nanny?" He pointed at the branches above us. "Up in a tree with the monkeys?"

We had a kind of gruff, semi-respectful masculine talk that went nowhere.

Along these dark and precipitous cobbled stone streets, the Indians are coughing, spitting out their lungs and waiting . . . for the white man to go away. In 141 years of independence, Bolivia has had 186 governments. The Presidential Palace is pockmarked with bullet holes from the last military takeover. The 16th-century Spanish iron gates have been repeatedly knocked down and ground paper-thin by the ceaseless tread of tanks. Every Bolivian I have met blames his country's instability on the lack of decent port facilities.

After Bolivia lost the war with Chile, the Chileans guiltily built Bolivia a railroad to the sea. After Bolivia lost the Chaco War to Paraguay, Paraguay built Bolivia a railroad to Brazil. And they go on complaining, the inhabitants of this heart-wrenching, bone-strewn land, perhaps the most beautiful I have ever visited.

The Bolivians give English names (taken from truck tires) to their favorite football teams: STRONGEST, ALWAYS READY

Delicate blue potato flowers in blossom across the bitterly cold and windswept Altiplano symbolize both the dichotomy and the harsh embrace between the unforgiving environment and the colorful, vulnerable but utterly durable civilization the Indians have created here. The Incas reputedly planted four hundred varieties of potatoes. They freeze-dried them. Now only eighty species survive.

The mounds of stones amassed over the years by generations of farmers. The back-breaking toil invested in these exhausted fields. Indians spend their whole lives walking. In ceaseless commute from one market to the next, they have become indefatigable walkers. Burdened with head slings containing heavy loads, they move at a steady pace, mile after mile, not unlike the Bedouin "walking machines" of the western Sahara. But the Bedouin warrior carries nothing but the curved dagger at his waist and maybe a pointed stick to skewer or swat away the vipers in his path. The bearing of cumbersome goods is left to his donkey, his camel, his woman.

Billy, the young American Peace Corps volunteer, returning to Bolivia after an absence of several years (his group was expelled), was moved to tears, as the ship approached Guaqui, by the sight of the Bolivian flag. Something strange, which he could not explain, happened to him in Bolivia, an experience which affected him deeply. He could not sit still or restrain himself from talking compulsively of his time here.

A day spent in the archaeological museum, examining ancient medical skills. *Los cranios trepanados*. The French writer Louis-Ferdinand Destouches, a.k.a. Céline, was trepanned following a serious head injury during WWI. Or claimed he was. The Bolivian police make inventive use of their whistles. They don't just blow, but are able to produce hoots and shrieks—like the cries of agitated birds and wild animals—fierce, commanding, sharp.

On one of the steep, slick, cobbled streets which vein the cliffs encircling this high-altitude city, I found myself in a large crowd of Indians. As motionless as they were quiet, I thought at first they must be listening to a speech, but heard no oratory voice. Then I realized the throng was not as silent as I had at first supposed. This was a second-hand clothes market I had stumbled upon, where young men circulated, bearing used sweaters, shirts, and trousers. Haggling over prices, the Indians conversed in whispered voices which I at first had been unable to detect. It took my ears some minutes to attune to their soft mutterings. There were hundreds of Indians, a babble of animated bickering, and a large turnover of old clothes in an atmosphere of profound calm, like the murmuring of doves. Seldom do these people raise their voices.

They sounded like a flock of sleepy birds, divvying up feathers. Llama foetuses on sale here. Also alligator oil. I stagger back to the hotel, loaded with bundles, and am arranging to have it all shipped back to Morocco.

Zézé, the witch-like Brazilian woman I met on the dock in Puno and drank beer with on the *Ollanta* during the overnight crossing of Lake Titicaca, is a follower of the *Macumba,* the Brazilian voodoo cult. She's beautiful and strong, but there was something eerily impersonal about her. Shining eyes dark and coldly bleak, like those of a snake, took in everything and gave back nothing. As one force—desire and curiosity—impelled me toward her, another—an intuitive voice inside my head—warned me to stay away. I learned the sparrow's nightmare, when it has lost the use of its wings as the serpent glides closer.

*January 7*

On the *ferrobus,* a kind of Disney contraption, a bus with its rubber tires taken off. It rolls on its rims on railroad tracks from La Paz to Cochabamba. $2.25 for the all-day trip.

The shadowy columns of the eucalyptus forest above La Paz, with bark-festooned branches, let down a flickering light. Cows on the watery green plain, cows reflected in rain puddles. The shadow-patched Altiplano—green going blue, with Andean snow peaks all about, like gigantic scoops of vanilla ice cream. I have to pinch myself—this is the high Bolivian plateau, and we are headed for the green center of the continent. The blue mountains, and the plain sweeping up into the clouds—a highway to eternity. The plain dotted by agricultural plots and cross-hatched with rudimentary mud walls and dwellings. Fuzzy sheep and an abundance of green grass. The *ferrobus* surges across a causeway dividing a broad and shallow lake, causing thousands of flamingos to take flight. Flapping frantically—an initially awkward but finally graceful pink mechanical caricature of a bird—they sail away over the high watery plain.

The empty lake is a desert of white sand where nothing grows. The sandy bottom, reflecting the unimpeded sunlight, yields nothing—deep water saturation ending in saline bitterness.

*Orura*

Another deadly one-dimensional mining community, where faces and lives appear as monochromatic as the russet ore scraped from the earth. The old old unbelievably old yet still serviceable steam locomotives. Indian women the shape and resiliency of rubber balls offer bread and goat cheese.

"*¡Helados! ¡Quesos! ¡Panes! ¿Que desea usted, caballero?*" a ten-year-old candy cutie speaks up.

And now, having traversed the high white plains of Bolivia, we descend through rock-strewn, pitted canyons leading to the great green riverine basin . . . but first the fine dust.

It is not altogether idle to speculate how I find my moods reflected in this rugged, magical landscape. The train tracks are twisted like sheep's guts. That jagged ridge could be the mandible of some colossal petrified monster. Sheep scramble up the crusty slopes. Mud cemeteries—mud to mud. *Aguas Calientes*—must be a thermal spring around here somewhere. Eucalyptus trees and more mud. The dark stream, meanwhile, grows clearer, the air by barely perceptible degrees warmer, we wind down from the naked heights. New and greener forms of vegetation. I, like that boulder poised on the precipitous hillside, have not yet taken that final and fateful plunge. Potential energy it is known as. Weight must be added to words. Cacti, some as big as trees. I must achieve a new angularity of language. Some funny-looking tree with a tapering trunk. Travel can trigger interior mechanisms, which cause a lock to turn after so many futile fumblings for the correct key. The creative observer must eventually turn his eyes inward, watch the shards falling slow motion into place, to form a pattern which is not at first and never easily discerned. Goats in a riverbed graze among red rocks beneath blue sky. And the Indians will insist upon tilling arid mountaintops, in defiance of reason and gravity. The mountains have flattened into hills, the riverbed has widened to one km—a broad tongue of pebbles.

Hills turning blue about sunset, hollows filling with deep shadow. Cotton, cattle, and cane. Run pig run! I too am on the run—not from but to.

*Nearing Cochabamba*

Now let us see why the Spanish Conquistadors chose this spot to found a city. (They must have arrived via the same river valley.) What lush countryside! (That's one reason.) Vegetation closing in. Oh, these blue, blue hills—they do not make me sad at all, but fill me with a lucid magnanimous joy. Indian ladies in comically high stiff straw hats lead fat cows home for the night. A Jewish cemetery, toy houses on a distant hillside, and an elegant spacious train station!

A Bolivian boy—or is he Brazilian?—lately from Palo Alto, California—says he studies at Stanford. I wonder. We met on the *ferrobus* and have a rendez-vous by the statue of El Condor de los Andes in La Plaza 14 de Setiembre at 8.30 PM tomorrow. Juan Carlos I think is his name. We're going to take in the Argentine circus we see advertised all over the city.

*January 8, Cochabamba*
*Hotel Cochabamba $36.00*

The bells jangle all night. They soothe my soul.

The hotel is located next to a church.

Cochabamba, like Arequipa, is another superior Andean town, with strong vestiges from the Spanish era. At almost the same altitude (8,000') as its sister city, with pure air and a warm but brisk climate, Cochabamba has been laid out in a dramatic, austere, but pleasing setting. Impressive colonial architecture, shops bursting with goods—especially the bookstores and stationers—and effective transportation services. The broad and elegant public squares immaculately maintained, the streets clean. The citizens, of both European and Indian stock, proud of their town, proud to be Cochabambinos, are cheerfully polite and enthusiastically welcoming.

A profusion of flowers, palms and eucalyptus dominates the parks. The surrounding region rich agriculturally—cheese, coffee, and especially the wine, all first class. Superb artisanal crafts, principally in leather and wool. An excellent, well-run hotel, similar to the Turistas in Arequipa, stands outside and above the town on a hill sloping gently upwards toward green mountains. An abundance of mountain water. Bougainvillaea, roses, and geraniums flourish in the subtropical climate. In a word, a remote but most agreeable town, almost exactly the same size as its twin in Peru.

Towns like Cochabamba and Arequipa possess a stability which their countries lack. Despite dramatic turnovers in the central government, political traumas, disasters and scandals in the capitals, the economic bases of these provincial towns remain secure. Before news has reached the provinces that yet another dictator has shot his way into La Paz, the new tyrant might have already been replaced, with little if any effect upon life in the rest of the country. In Cochabamba, the social rituals are well-entrenched, and the intellectual traditions persevere. These towns, due to their advanced ages and relative isolation, have attained a degree of wisdom.

Third-world countries such as Bolivia are viewed from abroad, mainly the U.S., as extremely unstable. This should be defined as politically unstable. Culturally, with centers like Cochabamba and the large industrious Indian population, they make the west seem comparatively fibrillative (death with twitches). This last statement must be interpreted, of course, as a purely romanticized view. One cannot separate cultural, political and economic realities. Furthermore, if Bolivia ever acquired effective political stability, we might soon see social upheaval. Many in the so-called advanced countries of the world would return, if they could, to the essential qualities of life that Bolivia has never lost—religion, simplicity, and tranquillity that slow life to a pace that everyone can keep up with, so that all can walk along together.

All this, admittedly, is pure speculation. All I have done is walk the streets of this city, talk to a few people, and catch glimpses of the vistas of the startlingly green countryside beyond.

Juan Carlos likes "everything white"—white bread, white rice, white sugar, especially white people.

As we drive along, the young, handsome curly-headed taxi driver accompanies the popular song on his radio in a passionate, tenor voice.

*"Maestro, al Hotel Cochabamba, por favor."*

*"Encantado, caballero."*

Now I begin to understand what the young man from the United States, the Peace Corps volunteer, wanted to express when he spoke so passionately of this country, attempting to articulate the "funny things" it did to people. (As he spoke, he licked nervously at the corners of his chapped lips, made cracked and raw by sun and wind.)

This poor, rugged, bewildered, landlocked country, with more governments than years of independence, possesses both touching charm and deep pathos. The humility of the Indian, the innocence in the wide brown face of the young policeman, and the ingenuousness which derives from being eternally poor, downtrodden and at the mercy of the elements, his fellow men included, reflect these human qualities. One feels the pain everywhere. In the stones that men have moved and shaped with their hands. In the fields. This pain touched the young American, causing him to weep at the sight of the tattered Bolivian flag. Now I too begin to feel the power of people without pretence and with not much hope. Toughness and cheerfulness make a fine combination. The Bolivians seem lacking in arrogance. The harshness of land and sky has left them little time for that; for arrogance, like any racket, is a time-consuming proposition. They take pride in their durability. It has given them their wisdom.

It is said that if the Indians were aware of the vastness of their numbers, they would instantly rise up and take back Lima (the Quechuas) and La Paz (the Aymaras). I wonder. I think they are well aware of their numbers, but don't see themselves winning in the short term, as an uprising would most certainly add to their misery. (And let's face it, their shanty towns already surround and nearly strangle these cities.) Deep down, they know they're going to outlast us all. Recently, there have been big oil strikes around Santa Cruz. The American technicians are pouring in to exploit the wealth. But when the oil dries up and the foreigners depart, the Indians will still be there, smiling over the land which they have regained by default.

*2.15 AM*

A dog is whimpering at the waning moon, or are those the cries of a lonely young woman in the next room? My imagination is running wild. I miss her too much.

*January 9*

Joy accompanies yet another departure at sunset. The shiny new bus leaves on time. This passenger is pleasantly tipsy, the pink sunset is draped over the horizon like layers of raw intestines, and from the street perfect strangers are blowing kisses and wishing me a safe and happy voyage. The seat next to mine is occupied by a bear of a man, also drunk. Will he, like a bear, snore? No, he only wants to rest his heavy, hairy, smelly head on my shoulder. Meanwhile the bus, with an accompanying fanfare of music, actually departs two minutes early.

"And at what time, driver, will the bus arrive in Santa Cruz?"

"At six o'clock in the morning."

"God willing. *Ojalá*."

"Of course."

Like heroes of old we glide away on the gleaming stallion (made in Argentina) through a shower of rose petals thrown down by the departing sun.

The word *ojalá* derives, I think, from the Arabic *Insh'Allah*. (God willing.) Words invoking the Muslim God still linger in the Spanish language.

*duranzo* = peach
*vainito* = bean
*tillo* = strawberry

This is spittin' country, and I mean serious. Blood, tobacco juice, rotten teeth, sputum swimming with TB and other nameless bacilli are loudly hawked and aimed in the general direction of the cuspidor but mainly straight onto the floor.

It is two o'clock in the morning, and a furry white puppy is gnawing on my leather shoelaces. Bear-man and I are sharing a bottle of pisco in a roadside cantina, somewhere in the mountains. Oh, my heart! There is the Southern Cross. Listen to the wind! The Milky Way as thick as cream.

"A woman is a man turned inside out."

This seems to be the extent of Bear-man's wisdom for the evening.

*January 11, Santa Cruz. Hotel Cortez $6.75*

We stepped off the bus into a wild wind full of dust. When it blows, the grit leaps into your lungs. The stately mango trees were thrashing their heads. I have seen cacti as big as maple trees. Four crops of corn a year, I'm told. One immediately notices the boom town bustle, and Juan Carlos says the women outnumber the men 8 to 1—the prettiest girls in Bolivia.

"The wind mad as Cassandra, who was sane as the lot of 'em."
—Ezra Pound, *Canto 72*

Faces in the clouds go scudding by, expressions shaped and borne by the wind. Faces of those deceased, including my own death mask, blowing in the wind. An entire fleet of sailing ships—Spanish galleons with high prows and towering sails, russet and yellow and pale blue in the fading day, are gliding across the Bolivian plain. The phantom fleet departs, and with the darkness the pall of sadness begins to descend, enveloping me in a finely woven cocoon of solitude.

"Blow wind blow. Blow sons and lovers apart." Where is she now—Tangier? Amsterdam?

Juan Carlos has come to Santa Cruz to visit his Auntie Tita, a handsome, brown-skinned widow of about forty who met us at the bus.

In the evening Juan Carlos and I go to the Parrillada Oriente Petrolero to play dice, consume juice-oozing slabs of grilled meat in the garden, and slake our thirst from huge green bottles of cold beer.

He teaches me a few words:

*virga, pinkilo* = cock
*arrecho* = horny
*chupila* = pussy
*corotas*= balls (in Cochabamba)

Juan Carlos described his departure from San Francisco. About thirty people came to the airport to see him off, family and friends, and he kissed each one in turn. The placement of his kisses ranged from ear to mouth, beginning with his mother's cheek, and ending with one planted on his lover's lips, causing his mother to scream.

His good-looking Aunt Tita, who I like very much, has invited me to tea in her impressive town house on the plaza. This little town of Santa Cruz, I am learning fast, has become one of the drug capitals of the world. There's an airport and

Juan Carlos's friends, who were shining shoes a few years back, now go about with satchels full of thousands of American dollars, with a revolver sitting on top. (Smith & Wesson the preferred model.) So much money changes hands that Main Street is now called "Wall Street." There are guns everywhere and so are the potholes, some as large as shell craters. The brand new, drug-financed Land Rovers and super Toyotas with huge tires and tinted glass have to winch themselves to safety right there in front of the church.

When Col. Fawcett visited Santa Cruz in 1913, he also befriended a widow, who told him "unwanted babies were left at night at the doors of the church in the plaza . . . to be devoured by the scavenging pigs that roamed freely in the streets. To stop this, the authorities had to banish the pigs—there was no holding up the supply of unwanted children!"

*Plus ça change . . .*

*January 12*

And I am becoming sick and tired of having to listen to or read their regulations, fill out their forms, stand in line, and tolerate this bullshit handed down by the cops, bureaucrats and military—everyone on the government payroll from the president on down who dole out the rhetoric, the red tape, the interminable forms and procedures one has to wade through in order to get anything done, in my case to buy a lousy train ticket! God, how it fatigues me, this throttling of the human spirit and stifling—as it is intended to stifle—enterprise, impulse, imagination, adventure, art—human instincts which make life bearable and even exciting. What a bunch of nameless assholes runs this show, and everywhere in South America it is the same. How did these fools get to be in charge?

500 LITTLE PEASANTS WILL BE ALPHABETACIZED THIS YEAR!
(Newspaper headline)

Visions for the novel:
1. Across the swampy plains and into the heart of a man who resides out there. 2. Within that heart exists a cold core of fear which has been transformed into a severe moral code. 3. Gain perspective on the man before cutting him down and patching him up. 4. The energy required to wade through a stinking vegetal morass in order to gain admittance to his lair.

A crowd of famished vultures surveys a dying mule.
They'll be doing us a service,
So please don't say it's cruel.

Reading Malraux's *Anti-Memoirs*. I like the way he throws it at you—one slightly off-center head-bumping statement after another:

"How to reduce to the minimum the 'comedian' side of one's nature." (I had thought Camus said that in his *Carnets*.)
"The obsession with sincerity is the pursuit of secrets."
"Admittedly the truth about a man lies first and foremost in what he hides."

*January 13*

In Montero, motorcycle taxis will take you anywhere in town for a peso, that is, if you like to live dangerously. The kids wait in the plaza beside a rank of shining steeds. The bus from Santa Cruz pulls in, and the passengers hop down as the kids rev their motors. They go shooting off, their machines raising rooster tails of dust, fares hanging on for dear life.

An impressive botanical garden here, which Juan Carlos and I visit on rented Hondas. A variety of trees offers shade and shelter from the hot wind that blows all the time—trees of such great size they must have originally formed part of the virgin forest which was chopped down around them. Paths have been cut through, cactus and orchid gardens laid down. A few docile animals—deer, gnu, tortoises, and the like—wander at will, fearless of jaguars who have retreated with the jungle.

I am developing a laborer's sunburn—neck, face, ears, and arms toasted brown; the rest white.

Sun Maid Raisins in small boxes—an effective laxative for the irregular traveller.

*January 14*

At times this trip amounts to an almost surreal indulgence in non-experience. Façades glide silently by as landscapes change (and are inter-changeable). Whole populations pass in the streets, but we do not exchange a single word. Trains, buses, jeeps, and motorcycles transport me from one unfamiliar yet oddly similar locale to the next. I pay my hotel bill and depart. I arrive and sign in. With a sign, the conductor shows me to my place. With a sign from the trainman, the engineer puts his machine into gear, and once more we are on the move. A sea of brown faces, a frothy ocean of Andean peaks angry with winter, the placid gray-green pond of the Altiplano . . . without making a ripple, I paddle through.

Does any of this belong to me? Unless I write it down, it all dissolves behind me like a wake following a ship. Tomorrow I set off for Corumbá in the Brazilian Matto Grosso and do not know where else, nor hardly care. Travel has become synonymous with the passage of time. As one day follows another, so does one town come after the next. Human contact has been reduced to the gaps of minutes, hours, maybe a few days. Hello, Juan Carlos, goodbye, Auntie Tita. I like you and your dog. Good morning, good afternoon, *hasta luego*. Please bring me a coffee, waiter, but don't make it too hot, because I'm moving on.

The planet turns, days pass, and nights are endured. The treadmill seems mine alone. Get out of bed in the morning and step onto a new stage. This traveller's most unique experience is that he never touches the world. I leave no tracks. My shoulder never rubs the wall. Will these barmen, conductors, and chambermaids remember me? Sunlight, wind, and rain are deflected by the invisible magic shield my mobility provides. From the mountains to the sea, from the jungle to the plains, following the courses of clear streams and brown rivers, I glide like an apparition, never remaining long enough in one place for my existence to be established.

And I am growing less capable of making distinctions. This park—does it remind me of the one in Paramaribo or in Cochabamba? When the parks converge in my mind, they form one green field. Which night, which day, which town and which highway? From where I sit, a web of roads radiates like spokes to the circular horizon. Making comparisons has become an absurdity; I am reminded at once of everything and nothing.

Like many an insecure traveller, I have lost touch with the original purpose of this trip, which was to hole up with my lady-love in some seedy but romantic South American port town and bang out a second draft of this novel. She's gone, and so is my desire. Not for her but for the damp sandwich of the typescript, the crispness and crackle gone out, which slumps forlornly in the bottom of my Spanish briefcase. The keys of my portable typewriter have rusted from non-use and lack of oil. Company at the end of the day relieves the pressure of writing, but not the company of strangers.

Brazil and Paraguay lie ahead, I think. Tomorrow means another random step with no implication of progress. Only the past linking with the future to force the present from its hiding place and onto the pages of this notebook.

Lines and lines. Lines to follow and lines to avoid. There are the tracks you were born on, but do not assume you will have the time to leap from your trolley to throw the next switch. Allah throws all the switches, boys. Or was it that indolent mestizo stationmaster half asleep in the shade of a mud wall, who without opening his eyes flips a lever with his bare brown foot, therefore altering your direction for all time?

Pablo Neruda on fate: "Every casual encounter is an appointment."

On the way to Auntie Tita's, I wandered the streets of this unfamiliar town, the empty white-hot streets of a Sunday afternoon. Auntie Tita wanted to give me something. I gave her a signed copy of my book. Juan Carlos had gone fishing with his buddies, and now she had something for me to take on my trip.

I turned left here sometimes right there, depending upon the general attractiveness of streets—attracted by an imposing portal, a movie announcement, an unexpected barrenness; or repelled by the stink of a dead dog in the gutter or to avoid a crowd of drunken Indians. At each intersection, I pondered between right and left or straight ahead. Will it make a difference? Will some accident befall me on the right, or will I be safer on the left? The street in front mirrors the one behind. The ones to the right and left look identical. I could flip a coin, but the odds predict more of the same to come. Somehow I arrived on time at Auntie Tita's door.

*January 16, Red Oriental Express*
*Santa Cruz to Corumbá, Brazil $6.75*

With the music coming down (a Spanish version of "Ghost Riders in the Sky"), and the rain blaring, this little train sets off across the great wet plain known as the Gran Chaco, for Brazil.

A fleshy brown lady with dangly gold earrings is my seat companion. We exchange weak, insincere smiles. In my absence, when I went back to the platform to buy a pack of cigarettes, she shoved my briefcase with the novel inside down the overhead rack to make room for her plastic sack.

The narrow-gauge tracks—so incongruously parallel in such raw surroundings, so shiny in the dull world—how mysteriously they conduct themselves across the watery plain. Sullen, bearded gauchos sit before their wattle huts. Isolated men on the rainy earth, beneath the muddy sky. Their melancholy cows move reluctantly off the tracks when the whistle hoots, then gallop violently into the bush as the train chugs by.

Lean black pigs graze in red puddles. How they love the mud. My companion has donned a red bandana and looks definitely gypsyish. She crosses herself—it is a bit spooky out there, where the great yellow rivers, like jaundiced serpents, feed off the land. A lumber camp—thick logs piled high . . .

This is the northern part of the Gran Chaco we are crossing—an extensive lowland plain, my guidebook tells me, divided among Paraguay, Bolivia and Argentina. Mostly arid land, dotted with stretches of dense forest and swamps during the rainy season (which is now). The highest temperatures on the continent have been recorded here.

Paraguay and Bolivia fought a bloody war here in the 1930's. Paraguayan settlers had originally opened up the region. Paraguayan soldiers pushed back the Indians. No one cared much about this wilderness until oil was discovered at the foot of the Bolivian Andes. Bolivia wanted access to the Paraguay River to ship oil to the sea. Paraguay refused to give up the lands, and more than 100,000 lives were lost in crude conflict. The war ended in 1935 with both sides exhausted. Three-quarters of Chaco Boreal or southeast Chaco went to Paraguay. According to my map part of that area is called "Presidente Hayes." Don't know why . . .

The thick-set man with the mustache, who was so friendly last week when I vainly sought to buy a ticket for this train, offered me a cigarette from his pack of L&Ms. Turned out he was a black marketeer, and we exchanged pesos for cruzieros. Smugglers everywhere and clandestine moneychangers are some of the most agreeable fellows you meet on a trip like this. Their racket, being so obvious and themselves so vulnerable to the whims of strangers, obliges them to be friendly. The logic is, I suppose, that the customer who is treated cordially is not likely to turn them in.

Wildlife:

The ivory-billed woodpecker flits from tree to tree;
In the stillness of the forest he turns to look at me.
His species are endangered, so they say up north.
Down here the people haven't been to school yet;
They don't know what he's worth.

The humming bird:

Here he's called the *picaflor,*
'Cause that's just what he does;
A master fertilizer,
Just like his friends that buzz.
The flowers get all rubber-stemmed,
When he hums around;
They open wide their petals,
And he enters without a sound.

The heartbeat of a bird
Is very seldom heard.

The wattle shacks along the tracks: women with narrow brown faces and children without much hope watch the train go by. My seat companion's butt is usurping my space . . .

In her sleep my fleshy friend has spread wide her legs . . .

In her odalisque dream, she displays a hairy armpit. South American Indians, like their Asian cousins, don't have much body hair. I count twenty or thirty.

Cacti here as broad as oak trees. Cactus fingers among the scrub. This is hawk and pigeon country . . . many varieties of the former . . . red-tailed hawks the size of turkeys.

Malraux:
"Europe believes that whatever does not imitate its reality represents a dream."

In India:
"Nowhere had I been so overwhelmingly aware of how much

all sacred art presupposes that those to whom it is addressed take for granted the existence of a secret of the world which art passes on without revealing, and in which it makes them share."

The bright and fragile cactus blossoms sit atop enormous dull green growths which appear as if they had been reared at the bottom of the sea from antediluvian roots upon which the true sun has never shone. At one time the Chaco, which we are crossing, was a sea. Dark flat-topped hills in the distance—I don't know what to make of them. Could these be the beginnings of the Ricardo Franco Hills which the explorer Col. Fawcett first saw in 1908, the description of which inspired his friend Conan Doyle to write *The Lost World*?

I spy a new kind of white-shouldered vulture. Herons take nervous flight over the misty wastes, like poor lost souls. This is mean country, ideal for predators. Every living thing out there owns spikes—spurs, horns, fangs, talons, beaks, thorns . . .

Now an invasion of yellow phoebus butterflies. Butterflies by the zillion flutter by. They go for the cattle droppings. Those turds, now golden with a myriad quivering wings, look as though they might take off. Where the semi-wild Brahmas have been grazing, the butterflies mass on the ground like a blanket of glittering yellow snow, agitating for a return to the heavens. Now they come inside the train.

The train has just collided with a magnificent Brahma bull and sent him sprawling in an explosion of yellow dust. The engineer slams on the brakes, and the rough-hewn male passengers instantly produce from beneath their dirty ponchos an array of evil-looking cutting instruments—machetes, sheath knives, swords, hatchets. Led by the train's cook, waving a meat axe, they leap out windows and doors, descend with war-yelps on the beast and start chopping him up, even before he has breathed his last. Triumphantly they return, lugging huge dripping chunks of red meat, wrapped in palmettos. The flies come in with them.

The tropics, meanwhile, are fast approaching. Air rank with the stink of blood, mud, vegetation and death is closing in . . .

A town, San José. The usual horde of impoverished vendors besiege the train. *Chicha* and chicken. The timid voices: *"¿Café? ¿Mangos? ¿Paltas? ¿Salteñas? ¿Empanadas? ¿Refrescos? ¿Limonada?"* A half-crazed six-gun-toting Franciscan priest roughly accosts one of the passengers and begins to babble in German. He's been out here too long. Off we go again through another cloud of butterflies. Dogs run after the train. It's a relief to be moving , even after a five-minute stop. Get away from that place, from that demented priest and his revolver.

Lunchtime: the soup, which contains peanuts, initially tastes good, but is quickly seen to contain a number of flies. Daintily, I spoon them to the rim of the plate. On to the next course. Meat, or is it? In God's name, *what* is it? It's . . . *moving*. Are those maggots? Nooo . . . on closer inspection I conclude it must be part of the bull that was just slaughtered, which part I dare not ask, flash-singed over the cook's wood-burning stove, and it's still . . . quivering! I forked the slab of half-live meat off my plate and catapulted it out the open window, where it was seized in mid-air by the jaws of a pursuing pariah. He wolfed it down in one gulp. Three different starches—corn, rice, and potatoes—are piled on a single plate. How could they have forgotten the yucca? Fortunately, I have this basket of Auntie Tita's own-garden-grown succulent stringless mangoes which she presented me as a travelling present.

Now we are entering a region of buttes, conical hills, and imposing red cliffs, home of the white-tailed hawk. Maybe this is *Lost World* country. According to Fawcett's *Lost Trails, Lost Cities*, that isolated, inaccessible plateau where dinosaurs might still be lurking is around here somewhere. The man behind me is making obscene sucking noises trying to dislodge a piece of meat from his crooked teeth. I lend him the plastic toothpick from my Swiss army knife which he accepts with a crazy, gap-tooth grin.

Every dead tree contains a bird of prey . . .

Approaching the frontier, we fall into the shadow of the giant—Brazilian goods on sale everywhere.

Cows wander at liberty through the streets of these towns. Indian cattle, Brahmas, behaving just like they do back home. My neighbor has woken up and chatters in a raucous voice with the other women. I liked her better asleep—fat legs spread wide, hairy armpit and all.

> "God is the loneliness of man."
>
> —Sartre

I don't think ole J. P. spent much time in this part of the world.

All the arguments about the existence of God are a futile waste of time. Of course, He exists—in the only place that matters, in the heart of man. Down here you learn that p.d.q.

Another lesson. Don't mess with a poor man's religion. It may be the only handle he has on a fate he finds bewilderingly brutal and indifferent. Tamper with it, or make him feel threatened—watch out—you may turn a meek man into a fanatic.

Entering parrot country now.

South America—your parks are peopled by your passionate

lovers, liberators and explorers—Bolivar, San Martín, O'Higgins, O'Leary, Fawcett, Prescott.

*Corumbá, Brazil. Hotel Santa Monica $8.00*
*Churrasceria Rodeo*

A distant spiral of black ashes, as though rising from a fire, fills me with a nameless longing. They're vultures.

Last night a rustic horse-drawn chariot transported me along dark and dusty paths from the train station to the hotel. This is a waterfront town. A high bluff overlooks the sluggish Paraguay River, scene of decrepit hulks rotting or rusting away in the gathering sudd. Crumbling warehouses, spectral customs sheds, and collapsing lacy girders all seem to have been put up in the same rubber-boom year—1910. Not much seems to have happened since.

Citizens stroll the palm-lined mosaic sidewalks, lean on the balustrade above the river, make light love and conversation. The African beat at once recognizable in the faces and music of the finger-popping Brazilians. Also many Bolivians who, having crossed the border looking for work, have taken up permanent residence. The town, however, belongs to the Arabs. Every other store is Casa Mustafa, Tienda Cairo, or Baghdad, Karim, Said, et al. Mostly Palestinians and Syrians. I see them reading Arabic newspapers, and listen in on their secret trader's language.

Corumbá—where Fawcett, age 57, set off in 1925, via Cuyaba, on his last trip into the interior. His aim was to find a lost Indian city, whose streets reputedly were "scented with vanilla, its walls lined with silver and gold," in a place he designated as "Area Z," somewhere in the Brazilian jungle. His fate remains a mystery, as neither his body nor bones nor any trace of the expedition was ever found.

Everywhere in Brazil you see prominently displayed the bigger-than-life official photograph of the president of the Republic. Dressed in evening clothes, a row of glittering medals on his lapel, a broad scarlet ribbon cutting diagonally across his chest—on his face an expression of arrogance is giving way to dismay. This could reflect a developing attitude toward his fellow-citizens. More likely, it will be with this haughty impatient mien that he will confront, upon returning home from a state banquet, the assassins who await him. The photo was taken by flash, and the eyes of the president squint in anticipation of the blast of light.

Otherwise, it's a rugged male population sitting straw-hatted before large bottles of beer in the outdoor cafés. Brazilians, like Americans, prefer their beer ice-cold, their meat thick, fast-grilled and rare.

I have been informed that river transport to Asunción is no longer available. Two comfortable steamers used to ply the Paraguay River all the way down to Buenos Aires, but nobody wants to travel that way any more, so the service was discontinued.

Down by the docks a man painting a boat—a moth-eaten old man, gold tooth in the middle of his mouth—told me that a small steamer may depart Saturday or Sunday, but I can't see myself waiting until then. My impatience disturbs me—an impatience fuelled by solitude. Probably it would be an interesting trip, but I'm in the mood to move on. So I've booked myself on the night train to Campo Grande. Tomorrow another ferrobus to Punta Pura on the Paraguay frontier. From there I'll make my way somehow to Concepción, where a boat for Asunción departs Saturday, so the old boy assures me.

| | —BOYS— | |
|---|---|---|
| You were born in? | Your name will be put on the list in | You will be conscripted in |
| 1955 | 1973 | 1974 |
| 1956 | 1974 | 1975 |
| 1957 | 1975 | 1976 |
| SECURITY OF THE FATHERLAND: Right, Honor, and Responsibility of Every Citizen | | |

Malraux:
"India is fascinated by the ceaseless flow of the Ganges, and the ever-changing face of the river."

*6 PM*

Sun caught in a crotch of hills sends out a blistering orange light, coating the plains of the Matto Grosso in a feathery pink gauze. A distant thunderhead also turning pink lets down a phallic stab of lightning, and, in histrionic response all the church bells begin to chime. Yes yes yes! One can see for miles. The Renaissance painters, taxing their imaginations to portray the elemental religious harmony between man and nature, therefore extolling the glory of the Lord, could not have done better. Whatever one is doing, one is in the act of becoming—becoming what, only time will tell.

*Ay-Oh!* in Brazil means *me.*

*9 PM*

And the thrill of yet another departure, this time aboard a

Brazilian train which will carry me all night across the swampy plain of the Matto Grosso. And the train leaves one minute early.

An Italian priest is pursuing me . . . they're all nuts down here. On this train everything goes without a thought straight out the open window—beer cans, garbage, etc. And now, you skinflint, you have been reduced to bumming, in the absence of friends, cigarettes from waiters, who in the hope of a decent tip cannot refuse.

*Midnight*

These moonlit plains, humped with the solemn forms of gigantic brooding animals—just hills asleep. I sit alone in my darkened compartment with the window wide open to the tropic night. The compartment resembles a roomy coffin with a window at one end, through which I witness the world of shades flash by. Life and death: two inseparable halves of an indivisible whole, and I'm half way there, maybe more.

*Campo Grande, Brazil*

This place has the reputation of a rough and ready cow town, where I was told the local machos pack six-shooters and don't hesitate to use them. So far I haven't spotted a single gun. All rather solid commercial middle class. With eight hours to kill between trains, I lounge in the park, doodle in my notebook and leaf through an old *Time* magazine I found blowing in the wind.

Brazil's coffee: first the fine powder is mixed with water in a saucepan and heated. At this point it has the consistency of chocolate sauce. Then it is poured through a cloth filter ("the sock"), and a little boiling water added. The tiny cups and saucers are kept in hot water and are placed before the customer with tongs. The sugar goes in first, followed by the coffee. The caffeine lift is electric.

This morning I saw seven dead cows decomposing in the sun by a barbed wire fence. The stench was unbelievable. Not a vulture in sight. Could the beasts have been poisoned?

Arabs dominate the scene here, too, so the rice is excellent.

The Brazilian Air Force sergeant (whom I observed in the railroad station) stands just over five feet tall. His sternness (his features locked into a permanent scowl), leanness (leathery, sunken cheeks), and diminutive size are summed up in the impressive jet black, impeccably trimmed mustache. The mustache gives this imp authority; the mustache says it all.

On yet another gleaming, big-windowed, air-conditioned *ferrobus (La Litorina),* we set off for another frontier. Like riding in an aquarium. I've got that snug feeling again, which only tramps and other solitaries experience, when all my bags are loaded and we are moving off together. In this part of Brazil, people of European stock are just as poor as the blacks and the Indians, no better off than their ancestors they left behind in the rural areas of Spain and Portugal to find a better life in the New World.

Mane of black hair flying, a girl in a bright red dress is running barefoot across a bright green field. Oh, the green green plains of the Matto Grosso . . . clean and fresh . . . and the red earth glows. Bands of flat-bottomed clouds parade in long rungs down the sky's wall. Fluffy green grass carpets the red floor of earth—sewn into the warp and woof of the land.

All my fellow passengers—businessmen, gauchos, old ladies,

teenagers—avidly read comics and movie magazines. As a writer, I should learn what the irresistible appeal of these "unedited photo-novels" might be. You guessed it—yep, it's sex.

Numberless grazing herds and endless grass—that's the essence of the Matto Grosso. Now I understand what the American settlers must have experienced when they headed west across the prairies in their conestogas. But one must not neglect the sky, for it plays a magnanimous sheltering role on God's stage. The grass exudes an effulgent light of its own, an illusion of a beckoning, ever-receding paradise. Yes, these plains do possess a radiance. Is that why I can see so far, or is the light playing tricks in the distance? Gentle rolling hills, ranged by young hawks . . . an illusion of tameness . . . in a heart of vastness. The friendly Brahmas, with their floppy ears, lend a placid, oriental flavor to the land, which one can hardly imagine without them.

Two bulls have fought by a water hole. The stricken loser lies stretched upon the muddy trampled earth, where he is guarded by the victor who stands on shaky legs, keeping at bay the hundreds of vultures which have assembled.

Last night on the train I was assailed by dreams so chaotic, with risky meanings utterly confused, summoning up childhood acquaintances like a crowd of the deranged. It was as though I had been born and raised in a nut house. What was the significance of this totally unexpected visit from people I had not thought of in 10 or 15 years? What possessed them to follow me down here? Will the subconscious never forget, like some jealous guardian of the past, never let go? A memory bank suddenly gone berserk, spewing out a newsreel of half-forgotten images. Why here? Why now? Who has dredged up these ancient episodes to make me feel guilty and uncomfortable in Brazil when all I wanted was a decent night's sleep?

Saddled horses tethered beneath a tree—the gauchos were holding a powwow. Nearby, a youngish woman in a faded pink dress waited by the well. Leaning against a fence, she held one hand behind her head in a faintly seductive pose. The scene looked like a cover of a cheap edition of an Erskine Caldwell-type cowboy novel—South American style.

Following a farewell sunburst, which illuminated the entire plain, darkness like a shutter closed out the day. I turned my attention to my fellow passengers. The man seated in front of me had a long livid scar across his sunburnt scalp, like someone whacked him over the head with a machete. The little fellow beside him must have been very proud of his thick crop of brown hair, for he kept running a comb through it, and primped the result with a caressing hand. He turned out to be a midget with a wizened face. He'd been joking and exchanging movie magazines with a lively young girl across the aisle. Her dark hair was bobbed; she wore a Levi jacket. I actually became jealous of the little fellow's success with her.

*January 17, Punta Pura, Brazil. Hotel Barcelona $5.00*

Cooler here, as they said it would be. Another decorated chariot, painted in many bright colors like an Andean truck and maintained in top shiny condition by the young driver, carried me along dark sandy paths, to the main street of the town—or towns—for a grass verge is all that divides two towns and two countries—Brazil and Paraguay—to my hotel.

LET THE GRASS DECIDE

A grass frontier
Strikes me as a good idea.
Let the grass decide
Who shall cross.

Later, looking for a place to eat and drink, I groped through the darkness toward a pool of yellow light and had my *aguardiente* in Paraguay. "Rose Garden" came over the radio in Portogee, taking me back to Amsterdam, winter of '71, when the tune was a hit and you never stopped hearing it. Madeleine and I were living in a room above a sex shop manned (sic) by a girl called Henny. It overlooked Kloverneersburgwal and was rented to us by a publican, Lodewyk, whom we had befriended while drinking beer (she—wine) and geneva in his bar. Munching apples and cheese, swallowing raw herrings whole, watching the seagulls come in for sliding, floppy landings on the frozen canal, I was warmed, in that unheated room, by the galleys of *Tangier Buzzless Flies* I was correcting for Athenaeum in New York. Madeleine's mother, the Baroness van Nagell, visited us in that room. She bluntly expressed her disapproval of me, what she presumed to be my life in Morocco, and that place we were living in—a tirade of criticism which only bound her daughter more closely to me.

*Chipahuasu*—a tasty green corn and cheese pudding which the barman insisted I sample. When you see Chivas Regal in gallon bottles lined up on dusty shelves in a bar not much bigger than a chicken coop, you know you're in smuggling country.

The easiest border I've crossed yet—two stamps in ten minutes. In Paraguay the military evidently handles everything, which due to increased efficiency is encouraging—discouraging in every other way.

The Paraguayan flag, except for a small seal in the center, is a copy of the Dutch:

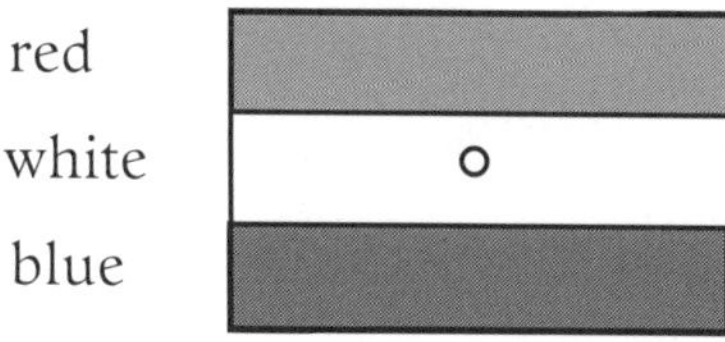


Another bus ride: $3.00

—PRICE OF CARGOES—

| | | |
|---|---|---|
| tomatoes | the crate | 50 |
| eggs | the box | 50 |
| potatoes | the sack | 50 |
| wire | the roll | 50 |

At the bus station, a fat woman in trousers, hair cropped short, kicked up one hell of a fuss over her baggage, which consisted of two brand new truck tires. She wanted to bring the tires inside the crowded bus with her, so she could roost on them, like a mother hen.

*On the bus:*

Sign on a hut the size of an outhouse: HOTEL. The usual elaborate necropolis on the edge of town. Now the dust comes in . . . The driver became so engrossed in conversation with his assistant he forgot what he was doing. Our speed dropped, and the bus began to buck in high gear. Sign before a homestead shack surrounded by blackened trees: A CORNER OF TEXAS. The flames had burned the dead trees into grotesque twisting shapes, like martyrs writhing on crosses. This washboard road is making my teeth chatter. Another control post, another police check, the 3rd or 4th within the last hour. Another pistol-packing, toothpick-sucking teenager sidled aboard to look us over. A jolly woman in bright city clothes sprinted out of the bush and leaped through the open door. Smiling at everyone, she fired up a half-smoked stogie. Beneath folds of loose brown skin, muscles like boards. Some of the passengers have brought along canteens. Wish I had one. The dust is coating my lips. I can taste the grit between my teeth. A young fellow who noticed me jotting down notes wants to know if I'm "writing a newspaper."

An old man attempted to strike up a conversation. He was either drunk, around the bend, or both. He spoke a few words of Spic, some Portogee. Guarani is the local lingo. One doesn't hear much Spanish. I was obliged to look through his military I.D. book. Born in 1916, conscripted in '32, discharged in '35 (dates of the Chaco War).

Black smoke spitting from its exhaust, churning up a cloud of orange dust, another bus bore down upon us like a berserk elephant. Half expecting a collision, I braced myself against the seat. Since the assistant moved to the back, the master drives recklessly. My guess is they've had a quarrel. The passengers look worried. Frowning, the assistant secures a package about to fly out the door. That beer in the last bar was one too many.

After a long, dust-eating chase, we caught up to and drew level with a truck loaded with yucca, corn, and bananas. The truckdriver, a boy about 13, gave us a surly look. He gunned his truck and caught up. He wouldn't let us pass. We're going to have a race.

A young passenger, her beauty made poignant by a face cruelly scarred by smallpox, has taken the seat next to me. The Guarani are generally a good-looking people—light brown skin, soft features, not heavy Indian. The driver has another companion to occupy his attention. The bus begins to buck once more. The Guarani greet each other with hands pressed together, as in prayer. The driver has been stung by a bee. The assistant takes over the wheel. Three pretty girls in an oxcart rolling along on wheels nine feet in diameter . . . three bright smiles.

*January 19, Concepción. Hotel Frances $17.00*

7.15 PM, 100°F. Never felt such heat. Humidity must be one hundred percent. Life here so sluggish, even the telephone wires are wrapped in moss. And they still talk about the Chaco War, as though it was fought yesterday. The Yanquis sold arms to both sides, I'm told. The hottest place so far, by far.

Why do I travel these barren roads? Why Paraguay and not Italy? Why Concepción and not Paris? Why this sweltering land-locked heat and not the breezy Med? Why impoverished lands whose past, present, and future have nothing to do with me? Why choose loneliness and solitude when I don't have to? Is it anonymity I seek? Is this what my wrecked family has done to me—sent me abroad to find some private haven from the storms? And where did I get this itch to write it all down?

The pace of life around here is oxcart slow.

Everything on this river seems to have been constructed in 1910—the crumbling warehouses in Corumbá, the Post Office here. Even my toilet bowl bears a 1910 patent. Mosquitoes by the million, so I am obliged to sleep beneath the net, which eliminates any possibility of ventilation. I'm dripping. Drink a glass of water, and it comes out right through the skin, as though I am a porous clay water jug. I can think of but one solution—strip, spread-eagle myself on the bed beneath the ceiling fan turned up to the max, and take frequent showers. My bathroom is a breeding ground for mosquitoes. They spawn in the toilet reservoir.

In Brazil, trying to get by with my wretched Portuguese became frustrating and tiresome. Upon entering Paraguay, I looked forward to the freedom and relief of speaking Spanish again. On a street corner in Concepción, I stopped to ask a policeman for directions. He sheepishly shook his head—no Spanish.

If I have a basic weakness or disadvantage as a writer, maybe it's because I've had it too easy. My parents' howling divorce notwithstanding, I haven't had to live with hate or fear, I haven't had to struggle financially. They gave me money, and I sailed away. Of course, there've been some rough crossings, but I've never lost my confidence. I've never been humiliated. I've done what I've done because I needed to do it, which was to leave my divorce-torn home, and writing, I discovered, soothed the wounds and was a way to stay away. I'm not a ship driven with sails reefed before a gale; I left the storms behind me. This schooner has been following a fair wind ever since it left home port. Of course, a ship wandering before a steady breeze rarely wins a race; then I've never thought of myself as being in one.

Good for good Chilean wine. A welcome relief from cheap beer and this rotgut *aguardiente* I've become addicted to.

The young travellers, mostly American, whom I occasionally encounter along the way—those who do not superciliously avoid all others, as if actually believing the landscape belongs to them alone—generally confine themselves to budgets lower than mine. As I dress simply, they take me for one of their own. However, when I reveal the name of my hotel, or when, from one evidence or another, they realize that economy is not my first concern, they can't quite figure me out, but as a rule grow more circumspect.

For the third successive night, my sleep has been afflicted by dreams. For the third or fourth time on this trip, my father has died. I make arrangements for the funeral and the burial, as I did for Ira (*dit* Belline) and her brother Ganya Bilankine in Marrakesh. I compose a eulogy, which I will deliver at the funeral. Madeleine places flowers on the casket. She wishes to say a few words, too, but, as I don't know what she'll say, I am filled with apprehension. This, in retrospect, surprises me: M and my father are very fond of each other. In my dreams I burst into tears every 10 minutes. Someone points out two bushmasters loose in the garden. This shocks, but it passes; there are more important things at hand. To my relief, I am able to compose my speech just in time for the funeral . . . when I wake up.

Pastora, the comely Indian maid (skin like milky milk chocolate, crinkly black eyes like raisins) who brings me my gourd of *maté* (Paraguay tea) in the morning, pads into the room trailing a faint sweet stink of female perspiration. I find the brew both refreshing and relaxing. If it's too hot, she insists I let it stand for a minute, for she doesn't want the silver straw to burn my lips. She shows me how to overcome the problem of drawing out the decoction without the straw clogging with weed. She tells me the brew contains the vitamins found in fresh fruit and vegetables. Her father, a gaucho who rarely sees a lemon, finds no nourishment in the drink.

He ran, and his running made him even more frightened. The properties we kids used to trespass upon. The old men who used to drive us off, as we laughed at them in fear and derision. They heard our insults but could not catch us. Swift legs carried us away over the fallen leaves. But now the other shoe has dropped. Now I am a landowner, of sorts—my puny plot of paradise in the Marrakesh oasis. Writers should never own property. Shouldn't build houses. It distracts them from the main job. Leafing back through the years to my cantering boyhood, I recall those days when I was the stealthy runner, the swift intruder, and the impudent offender of age and manners.

Now reading *Pigeon Feathers* by John Updike.

Five hundred boy scouts in Concepción on an outing. They came up here from Asunción in a navy ship. They camp in the park and swim in the river. At dusk we followed the girls down to the waterfront where they flirted with the sailors and danced on the riverbank to the rock music blaring from the ship's loudspeakers. On Saturday morning the boy scouts marched down main street. "Left right left," they chanted. Little kids, guys bigger than me, old men with beards who carry the flag—all boy scouts.

*January 20, 4 PM. On board El Presidente Stroessner (\$16.00 for a 1st class cabin) bound from Concepción to Asunción on the Paraguay River*

The ship is scheduled to depart in half an hour. I lie on my bunk and look through the open door at the river bank opposite. On a green sward four horses are pulling a blue wagon. A large box sits in back. It's a coffin. A stray horse follows and a naked boy aboard a mule. In these parts, the horses know how to stand quietly in a skiff while the rivermen do the rowing. The ship's horn sounds—once. I welcome such flash encounters with scenes I let my imagination interpret.

The horn blasts again—twice. The ship begins to tremble in anticipation of another departure.

Released of cables, the ship noses upstream, makes a wide turn and then, in the grip of the current and the accelerated pulse of the screw, shoots down past the waterfront. The lines of people waving are children. The 1910 warehouses, like old photographs viewed in bright sunlight, gradually fade from view.

Updike would make a model prisoner. Evidently he can withstand—even thrive upon—confinement to small quarters for extended periods of time. His examinations of cloacae so detailed you wonder if there's any shit left in the sewers. A brilliant writer and precise observer, but God every ten minutes I've got to jump up from my bunk, run outside the cabin, and lean over the rail for fresh air. How long can he hold his breath? Or does he write in order to breathe?

These binoculars enable me to intrude into other people's lives. Now I'm focused upon a typical riverine establishment—unpainted board shanty, thatched roof. At the edge of the river stand the listless children. They wave as the ship passes, but their hearts aren't in it. Behind the children, dressed in a dirty pink frock, stands the woman. Behind the woman—dark breeches and a dirty undershirt—sits the man. All barefoot. They too watch the gleaming vessel slide by but do not wave. Horses stamp beneath a tree. Cows wade through the scrub. The dog barks and bounces with excitement, but the adults do not move. Have they been frozen by the repeated sightings of the immense white ship slipping powerfully by? Do they detect something in the affluent, gaily dressed passengers that immobilizes them? These questions my binoculars cannot answer. The scene rapidly recedes into the bush, is swallowed for all time (my time) by the dull green void.

Pale birds at dusk. Cranes. Broad wings flapping across the river. Flecks of light in the primeval gloom. The gloom swallows all. A great hawk watches from a dead limb. The wake of the ship breaking along the bank causes a herd of drinking cattle to stampede.

*11 PM*

All these bodies, sprawled over the metal deck, exposed to wind and spray. Nothing more than a blanket or a strip of canvas insulating them from the humming steel. They sleep and sleep, summoning up for me Conrad's description of the pilgrims aboard the *Patna*. I've walked all over this ship. I've mounted the ladders and trod all three decks. One old woman in her hammock . . . she lies within, withered thing, chrysalis-like, a mummy within its shroud. They sleep while I, wide awake a few feet away in my air-conditioned cabin, think and write of them. Who assigned me to be the midnight chronicler of the dull and dead? I'd like to sleep soundly with my head resting against boiler plate, but I can't. Or can I?

The young waiter. He has served me all over South America, usually in the better bars and restaurants, which bestow on him that essential bit of pride. He's 23 or 4 or 5, good-looking too and knows it, and he's a bit simple-minded to boot. He enjoys his job and appreciates the tip. He has the youthful energy and the agility to be everywhere at once. His swiftness enables him to linger longer. He wears a smile and has good hands and seems to care. Without ever having exchanged more than a few words with him, I wish him luck. I hope he doesn't turn out like the older waiters, who let him do most of the work, the pot-bellied ones who don't give a damn any more and haven't even bothered to shave.

*January 21, Asunción. Hotel Guarani $95.00*

Whirring and whistlings in the park—Plaza de los Heros—produced by some insects up in the trees. Cicadas which, according to an aged member of the shoeshine brigade, appear only during *el tiempo de sandia,* "the time of the watermelon." January is melon-season here south of the equator.

The street in front of the hotel is lined by a row of wooden crates where local women sit before baskets of fresh fruit and vegetables. Mostly they are venerable old dames, very competitive, calling you *guapo* and *rubio* in pseudo-seductive tones to lure you to their stalls. The one on the end is manned by a much younger woman dressed in a kaleidoscopic outfit, dazzlingly bright orange and blue stripes, with headdress to match. She saucily smokes a pipe and wears a monkey-tooth necklace around her neck. I bought my mangoes from her neighbor. As I walked away she called out in an appealing but strangely imperious voice, "Next time you buy your fruit from Mariana."

In front of every bank is a garden; in each garden loiters a legion of young men. Average age about twenty. With fake leopard-skin briefcases bulging with money, they accost any passer-by who exudes the slightest whiff of affluence. Old ladies write out checks on the tops of walls. Tourists sign traveller's checks on the backs of obliging shoeshine boys. (For a small tip a shoeshine boy will lend you his back.) The shoeshine boys attend, like languid servants, the money-changers and their clients. The official rate of exchange, which has not been adjusted in 10 years, has become something of a joke. Only the most naive tourists, or businessmen up to their necks in debt to the state, make their transactions in banks. The American banks, the English, Dutch, Brazilian, and Argentine banks—more business is transacted in the parks than behind the cool, plate-glass windows. The hinges on the doors are becoming squeaky. Spiders proliferate in the corners. The tellers are falling asleep. The young men with the fake snake-skin and leopard-skin bags have usurped the money trade. Could these fellows cause a financial revolution? After all, they're eager young entrepreneurs making the best from the economic stagnation perpetrated by the cobwebbed rigidity of laws no one observes.

Jasmine grows in profusion along the wall surrounding the French Embassy. The heavy scent it throws out after dusk makes me long for our hot African nights when Madeleine and I stayed up late in the outdoor cafés of the Ville Nouvelle of Marrakesh, Marechal Lyautey's gemstone of the French Protectorate of Morocco.

Pipe-smoking Mariana has a posture like a guardsman. When she stands up, balances the basket of fruit on her head, and parades in front of the hotel, the moneychangers hoot and whistle like a crowd of wild beasts in the forest.

*January 22*

I just shredded my thumb on the suitcase catch. This old suitcase of my father is on its last legs. This is leather land, and I need to buy another.

Col. Fawcett, passing through Asunción in 1908, was entertained by one Cecil Gosling, the British consul. Gosling later settled in Tangier, where I knew his widow. She lived in a rambling old house on the Sharf. During lunch, while she spoke of her husband's adventures in South America (she lent me his book), the chickens and the ducks used to wander in from the garden and peck at the crumbs under the table.

The Botanical Garden. Two-headed cow foetuses in bottles, snake skeletons, monstrous armored beetles, tarantulas, scorpions, foot-long poisonous centipedes. The foetus of a whale—a tiny thing contained within a vial. And here in land-locked Paraguay, the eye of a full-grown whale—a hideous pulpy object which stares dully from a huge transparent vat. In another vial I spot a *candiru*—the evil little river fish that desires to swim up the orifices of man or beast and there, for reasons best known to itself, to lodge itself with downward-pointing spines. About three inches long, it has a sharp snout and forked tail. The curator tells me it was extracted from the penis of an Indian.

A scaly ball in the center of a cage—what is it? A sleeping armadillo.

Hard to say how old Mariana is—14, 18, maybe 24? Girls mature quickly here in the tropics. They marry early and have children early. Like many Guarani women, she exudes a force and mystery that emanates mainly from her dark skin, her languid energy, the centuries of cruelty and suffering associated with Spanish dominance, and the hard lot of women in general. Now I buy all my fruit from pipe-smoking Mariana. She seems to sense she has a bit of a hold over me, or at least over that part of my wallet that goes toward the purchase of mangoes. She has a brother in the leather trade. So this afternoon she will take me to look at suitcases, as the one my father gave me has completely worn out. I have to tie it together with rope.

*January 23*

Being so completely out of touch—(except for one letter from Madeleine) no mail in two months —has placed me in the category of an intimate stranger to myself. Encountering only unfamiliar faces, I am obliged to a certain extent to place my trust in them. The one I have the most faith in knows as little about me, as I of him. He doesn't know the names of those I love. He may have a vague outline of where I come from and an intuition of what might befall me next. Given that objectivity which only a stranger can bring to focus, he may know me better than I do myself. He's my railroad-station bus-depot green-park buddy.

Excluding him, I have for the most part lived outside the pressure of personalities. (My railroad friend is mainly content to listen.) My days of solitude have assumed a certain blandness. Taxi drivers and shoeshine boys demand to be paid; it is easier to pay from the pocket than from the heart. I feel out of shape and perform callisthenics and yoga exercises on the hotel-room floor. I float I fly I sleep late because I have read all night; only the maids know the hours I keep. In this town, like all others, nobody knows my name. It has been written down on a slip of paper here and there, but with the exception of my green-park companion, not a soul is aware of my true identity.

To be sure, a certain anxiety assails me from time to time. I don't know what anybody else is doing. Lacking letters, cables and telephone calls—those urgent communications—I feel almost virginal in my ignorance of basic facts. This goes for the world as well. Except when I catch a glimpse of a Spanish headline, it rolls on without me.

*January 24*

I have travelled across this continent with a sheaf of introductions I haven't used until now. The day after tomorrow, or the day after that, depending on the weather, I am being flown by small plane into the bush as a guest of the Anglo-Paraguayan Cattle Co.

The War Museum displays a secret weapon from the Chaco War—the fork of a tree. Thick straps of red inner-tube rubber have been attached; they join in a leather pouch large enough to hold a hand grenade. I can imagine the Paraguayan soldiers' excitement as they put the thing together (as country boys, they must have all known about slingshots), and the Bolivians' horror when a bomb landed in their trench.

I have noticed that Mariana carries some flab on the backs of her upper arms. What look like stretch marks radiate to her armpits from her heavy breasts. I must revise her age upwards . . . 25, maybe older.

Experience as fantasy as experience.

*January 25*

Even in anonymity there can be tenderness. I was surprised, almost shocked, when, yesterday evening, in a shop where I had stripped to the waist to try on one colorful, hand-embroidered Paraguayan shirt after another, Mariana allowed her hand to stray across my naked shoulder, sending a shiver down my back.

Back at the hotel, I admired the matching pair of belted leather suitcases, one slightly larger than the other, handmade by her brother José, and pasted on the colorful stickers I've been saving up from all the hotels I've stayed in.

*January 26*

When I talk to my father on the phone, which is every month or so, his message never varies. "Everything about the same here, not much news, everyone's fine," etc. I call my father not my mother because he lives alone. He hasn't remarried, his life is smaller, he needs me more, and he worries more. Although I have seen some amazing sights since we last spoke, have had an adventure or two, my own laconic reports mimic his own. I have no news of anyone but myself, which is really what this diary is all about. There is really no news at all. Were there news, I would have to describe it as a subtle release—if only a temporary one—from the human realm, where blood flows, where people throw their arms about one another, either in embrace or in struggle. If I have made any progress, I could not begin to describe it in an expensive, long-distance telephone conversation. Some time from now, the answer might fall clear, as sunshine radiates from behind departing clouds. For the present, suffice it to say, as I dutifully report to my father, my health is strong, spirits high, outlook good, and I am determined to finish the trip. That I am often bored and lonely and haven't done a lick of work on my book I do not report.

The tall black Brazilian who speaks with his hands. See the long black fingers, listen to what they say.

A final visit to Mariana's stall, where she presents me with a basket of fruit to take to the Chaco. Gifts of fruit must be a South American custom. She's more reserved now, knowing that I am leaving. Two twists of black tobacco, coiled like snakes or turds in the bottom of the basket. They exude a rank odour. Presents for the gauchos.

*January 27*

*Tuperandá* (Place of God) Ranch. 500,000 hectares (1,250,000 acres).

From the Cessna, the vast green prairie looks as unmarked as a billiard table, now and then embellished with the blue-brown signatures of the rivers, ornate as Arabic script. They look a little like this. We have been given a buzzard's eye view of the Gran Chaco.

Cranes take wing when the plane comes in for a landing. Brahma cows seven feet high at the shoulder will stampede at the sight of a man on foot, the pilot warned. They are accustomed to mounted men only, he said, and to watch out for fighting bulls.

On the grass airstrip Guarani women offer cheese and honey. Vultures over the swamp. A tall, lean, blue-eyed man, his face deeply lined and burnt by the sun, came over and stood in front of me. Umberto Hack, he introduced himself as, with mingling conviction and politeness, which was how he offered each statement. Ranch manager. Swashbuckling gaucho outfit—baggy trousers, greasy leather chaps sewn with silver ornaments, fringed leather apron with bright-colored strips of cloth wrapped around his waist like a cummerbund. Jangling wheel spurs, revolver on hip, wide-brim straw hat, sweat-stained.

A servant led forward two horses and we mounted up. A pair of stone bolas attached to a braided leather rope was looped over his saddle horn. A rifle butt protruded from its sleeve. I began to wonder about this display of weaponry, just to meet a plane.

As we rode along, he talked forcefully of the plains and of the men who live out here, and of the wonders of space. Those faded blue eyes—faded perhaps by an intensity of light which his German ancestors, when they settled these lands, must have found oppressive—swept the prairie as he babbled in stilted but perfect Spanish. He belongs to perhaps the strangest race of all, one addicted to both art and violence, whose more rigid characteristics, I thought, may have mellowed after years in this tropic land. In Brazil I had already observed people of European descent to be as poor, sloppy and dirty as their dark-skinned brethren. Stripped of "the fatherland" and removed to another, to which he referred repeatedly as *La Patria,* which provides no easy answers but presents many challenges, men like Señor Hack have been able to shake off their stiff heritage and relax . . . maybe. He was born out here and reacted contemptuously when I told him about the old-timers from the old country who were continually coming up to me in Asunción to ask if I speak German. I suggested that his baggy trousers might derive from the Moroccan *sirwel* you see every day in the streets of Tangier and Marrakesh.

"Well, what do you expect?" he said. "The Spanish were *moros* for 700 years, a fact which should never be forgotten!"

We passed by the gauchos' shacks. Señor Hack said they ride out at three o'clock in the morning to beat the heat. By two PM, having already worked ten hours, their day is finished. Holstered six-shooters slapping thighs, they were playing soccer with their children in front of the shacks. The gauchos are poor and bullets expensive, enforcing judicious expenditure. Señor Hack snapped out orders, handed out my house present—pungent rope tobacco. No question who's in charge here.

The hacienda more English than Spanish. Two-storey wooden frame. He showed me to my room. No wife in sight, but was there one? These chintz curtains . . .

Dusk—there isn't any. Here in the Gran Chaco the night slams the door on the day. Before supper, serenaded by a million shrilling insects, we sipped Scotch on the verandah. The real thing, Dewar's—not the Argentinean crap—diluted with water from the well. When I mentioned I am a writer he declared in a passionate voice his love for literature and ran to bring me two books—Conrad's *Victory* and Hardy's *The Mayor of Casterbridge.*

He wanted me to sign them.

I said they are not my books.

He insisted—he wanted a writer to sign them.

I signed.

Dinner, served by a white-gloved Guarani woman. Señor Hack likes his food. Duck, from the river, garnished with slivers of mango and avocado from my gift basket. The duck tough but tasty. Rice. A bottle of ice-cold Chilean wine that's been down the well. His music is Mozart.

Suddenly, he stood at the table, shot me a stabbing glance which I was unable to fathom, left the room and didn't come back. I nibbled the watermelon by myself. I asked the woman, where is Señor Hack? She made a noise like the sound of wings flapping and smiled. She spoke only Guarani. I poked around the house looking for him, but there was no sign of my host. He'd gone.

*January 28*

Dawn. The crickets cranked their wild motors, then fell silent. Señor Hack and I saddled up and rode out. No mention of last night. These wide plains, brooded over by vultures and great birds of prey, attacking a new-born calf, pecking its eyes out. Wild turkeys *(chajha)* hooted across the swamp.

The solitude of the swamp, the loneliness of the plains, the gloomy silence of thick forest where jaguars lurk, and above all the oppressive heat drags me down and drowns me in the heavy monotony of heat-drenched nature. Rustlers hold out in various pockets of this vast ranch, Señor Hack said. He shoots them on sight. As a counterpoint floppy-eared Brahmas stared pacifically as we rode by. Screaming water birds protested our intrusion into their swampy domain. Rolling on wooden wheels nine feet in diameter, ox carts hauled logs from the swamp. Spiderwebs as broad as tennis nets. I'd forgotten how much I dislike horses and horseback riding. Crotch already rubbed raw. No feeling of confidence or control. Señor Hack in the saddle: an impressive sight. The man and horse as one. No wonder the Aztecs were terrified of Cortez and his mounted, armored conquistadores. No daylight between his butt and the saddle, even at a full gallop.

Surprised by our horses, a family of rheas raced across a field of blackened stumps. With a war cry Señor Hack took off after them. These Paraguayan quarter horses accelerate like a motorcycle. I gripped the saddle horn and hung on for dear life. He already had his bolas out, swinging them like a loaded lariat. Eating dust, I tried to keep up. My horse got hit on the head by a flying rock. He shied sideways and nearly threw me. I lost one of my stirrups. The horse was bleeding.

By the time I arrived on the scene Señor Hack was ready for the kill. A pale, gray feathery ostrich-like creature, its legs entangled by the bolas, lay on the ground looking up at us with big bewildered eyes. Señor Hack cut its throat with an evil-looking knife he kept concealed somewhere on his person. He wiped off the blood on the leather apron. The rest of the rheas stood in the distance watching, wondering . . . why?

*January 29*

A heavy lethargy has engulfed me. I feel like a half-collapsed balloon. Formless—yet with room for a renewed dimension; slack but with the possibility of tautness; grounded—but still with the potential for flight. I sleep and sleep. I can barely raise myself from the bed. When I wake, I read, which puts me back to sleep. When I go downstairs, I eat, which only makes me drowsy. The heat . . . 100° . . . constant, day and night—it never seems to abate. A porous clay jug keeps my drinking water cool. I am bathed in the now familiar patina of perspiration.

There are English books all over this house. Someone

does . . . or did . . . a lot of reading here. Señor Hack hasn't uttered a word of English. Then who?

This balloon has run out of gas and has come to earth, albeit gently, on the vast plain of the Gran Chaco. Surrounded by cows, fenced in, laid low by the heat and humidity, no radio and no plane until tomorrow, at the earliest, I am only able to maintain this diary through the dreary force of habit. No, wrong—these words not only console me, they are actually waking me up. I have just laid down my book. For the first time in two days, I am wide awake. Belief in my writing handpumps the deflated spirit.

This morning the tractor broke down, stranding us in the swamp. Ibises and spoonbills, taking wing through the dead trees, filled the forest with departing cries. Mosquitoes drilled through the denim. My blood, mined by the insects, splashed over my wrists and arms. Amidst forlorn hoots from the trees, foxes and armadillos scuttled past. The shy beasts—always in such a hurry!

These bouts of restlessness and inertia, when I have sunk to the depth of believing in the uselessness of any endeavor, any expenditure of energy—even that required to raise my sluggish body from these saturated sheets—often presage a period of renewed clarity of purpose, a solution revealingly suggested, which will drive me to fresh examinations, new encounters with myself, maybe.

Tonight, after supper, Señor Hack asked me to read some of my work to him. I didn't have any copies of my books with me, having already given them away, only the unfinished manuscript of the novel I have been dragging all over South America. I carried down the old Spanish briefcase and dug it out. Haven't looked at it in weeks.

I began . . . didn't know how much he was taking in. I hadn't heard him utter a word of English since I've been here, but I thought . . . this isn't so bad . . . it's better than I thought it was .

. . hopes for the future . . . renewed interest in my own writing.

When I took a breather, reached for the glass of whiskey to wet my whistle, I saw tears in his eyes. I was perplexed and almost shocked. There was nothing emotional in what I had read, just an opening description of a seedy South American port town, an amalgam of places I visited in Guatemala three years ago. Suddenly I realized it's not my book that produced this reaction, but the fact that someone was reading to him. Our eyes met, and a kind of unspoken secret passed between us. Someone else preceded me in this chair. Someone else's voice read those novels to him.

He got to his feet and left the room. The next day the Cessna took me back to Asunción. I never saw him again. I'm not even sure he sleeps in the house.

*January 30. Back in Asunción*

We were entertained by harp and guitars in an outdoor café. As a coarse reminder of where I am, Mariana averted her head and spat heavily on the ground. Mango-girl chews tobacco as well as smoking it.

The man at the next table had a green arm: green from being shoved up a thousand cows' asses to feel if they are pregnant. Fanaticism: proof that sincerity carried to extremes ultimately leads to madness.

Everywhere in South America manners are good; they advance the spirit of human contact. No one says *adios*—that would be too final. All say *hasta lluego* (see you later), even the stationmaster who slams the door to your departing train.

On the wind-swept plains, I have experienced certain tremors. In the depths of the swamp, I only feel foreboding—a warning from the water. On the lonely trails across this continent, I have received, from time to time, implicit hints about where they are leading. Just as they have drooped, like thirsty flowers, within the dreary confinement of hotel rooms, my spirits soar while on the road. I hardly know whom to thank. In the solitude of night—a beach, a dusty lane where I am the only walker, along the back streets of Lima—I have known a definite but fleeting bliss. The cry of a gull, the sea's weary mutterings, whining Indian music drifting from a cantina, wind—these sound effects make me more acutely aware. Dusty soil binds my feet to the moon. In the desert, where blowing sand can be counted upon to erase the past, I feel a surge of magnanimity. Jealousy expires, fear dissolves, selfishness evaporates, frustration becomes a melting memory, and I know compassion.

*On the bus. Asunción to B. A. 18 hours, $13.00*

Now, I've travelled on many buses—Moroccan buses, Portuguese buses, London double-deckers, Greyhounds, Central American buses, Fifth Avenue buses, Peruvian buses—but never before has whiskey been served to me on a bus. Argentine scotch, to be sure, but a couple of shots at six o'clock in the morning does a man good. Three truck drivers splashing naked in an irrigation ditch flash toothy grins from beneath bushy mustaches. I drink to those fellows.

In Paraguay and in northern Argentina you see a lot of 1949 and 1950 Mercurys. Model A cars and trucks still very much in use, reminding me of Mimi, my dad's beloved old Model A coupe with a lever to advance the spark, the one that burned up in the garage fire back in 1946.

Rosario, where we stopped at a restaurant in the middle of the night: baths *(baños)* for gentlemen *(caballeros)*, baths for *damas,* baths for children 3-8.

*January 31, B. A. Hotel Lancaster $115*

After Bolivia and Paraguay, B. A. glitters like Paris, Rome, and London all rolled into one.

Unexpected brilliance from the sky illuminates distant scenes. Symbols spread like weeds and shoot up like trees. The orange lights of the harbor illuminate the intense activity on decks. Sex in the streets. Plenty. Painted women surge forward and block my path.

In *Roma*, Fellini demonstrates how the mass of humanity, a few bright faces excepted, repeats—and is doomed to repeat —the lives of their ancestors. Rome is the stage, and the show goes on. A herd of sometimes beautiful pigs whose basic message is: "Oink, we're human, so why should we give a shit about anything? We want beds, we want women—and they don't have to be pretty to please us—we want food and wine and entertainment and occasionally some rest. These are our demands and they must be satisfied."

Anybody who has seen a herd of pigs being fed knows what an ear-splitting racket they make when fighting for food.

*February 1*

On the surface at least, B. A. appears to be one of the most luxurious cities in the world. The big department store around the corner is called Harrods. The streets are lined with dozens of others, equally stylish and sumptuous. Brilliant English language bookshops. Shoes and leather coats made to order in 24 hours. Everybody well-dressed. The girls sexy, stylish, gorgeous. The men good-looking and well-turned-out. Spanish spoken with what sounds like an Italian accent. Peacefully beautiful parks and gardens. Traffic and pollution moderate this time of year as it's high summer, and a percentage of the population has left town, gone to farms in the country, or to the beach.

The other side of the coin, hidden from the eye,, is just around the corner. This morning's paper describes how yesterday's rain and high winds (which began to blow just as I reached the hotel) collapsed a factory wall onto 27 "precarious dwellings" of a shanty town, killing 17. The shanty-town dwellers were reported to be sleeping (7.30 AM) at the time, and the few witnesses said they first saw sheets of aluminium and zinc fly over. Then the wall (100 yards long and 45 feet high) collapsed, burying many people under tons of rubble.

"'Get me out of here, I can't stand it any longer,' was a cry heard from under the debris. Some of the victims were brought out mutilated and unrecognizable, while several children appeared unhurt after being trapped for hours."

*Febuary 2*

In most South American capitals the shoeshine boys (or men) normally kneel on the pavement or sit on a low stool while the client occupies a comfortable throne-like chair. In B. A. the situation is reversed. Here the shiners of shoes and boots roost on upholstered benches surrounded by an exotic array of fluffy brushes, innumerable shoe ointments, polishes and pomades, while the customer is obliged to stand with one shoe on the box, thereby shifting most of his weight to the other foot which, after hours of walking the streets, I found agonizing.

As he whisked the dust away from my shoes, the old fellow looked up and inquired optimistically if I were a sailor. (B. A., a port, swarms with boys in blue.) To oblige him, and to hear what he had to say (for the phrasing of certain inquiries hints at a flood of information itching to be released), I said

I was. Passenger ship or cargo? As I am in the habit of reading freighter manuals in the hope—so far, vain—I might one day board one, I reply cargo. Have I ever had a Japanese girl? I haven't, but say I have, with an appropriate gesture of lasciviousness. Ahhh! And he made the international male fucking sign, touching together thumb and forefinger of his left hand to form a circle, and jabbing hard through it with the middle finger of his right. Do I know Barcelona? I've been there a couple of times, don't really know the city, but say I do. And Bilbao, Yokohama, Sydney, where he has left behind a legion of "nephews." Turned out to be a Spaniard from Burgos. My foot, meanwhile, was killing me. He ordered me to switch shoes, which I did, willingly. He was almost totally deaf, heard nothing I said, just wanted to relive his sailoring days, and those one-night stands with Japanese, Spanish and Australian girls. His memory whirling, he lingered over my shoes, polishing and brushing even the leather laces.

The old-fashioned Mercedes buses, with their snubby noses and shiny elaborate grillwork, convey an impression of pre-World War II solidity, when sturdy German machines bore an untarnished reputation for reliability, before humanity learned what German machines could do to them.

*February 3*

*¿Queso fresco? ¡Que fracaso!*

*February 4*

Faces in a crowded gallery on the docks of Buenos Aires, where I waited for passage by hydrofoil to Colonia, Uruguay, delayed by bad weather. (We have already set out once but were forced to turn back by high winds and rough seas.)

Four hours of idleness: I am condemned to waiting-room detachment, studying my fellow passengers with a superficial eye and re-reading a letter from Madeleine.

We spent half a year in New York. She was not allowed to bring her daughter with her. Julie stayed behind in Holland, to be looked after by Martin's sister. I managed to complete my novel, *Tangier Buzzless Flies,* and we travelled for a month in Guatemala. But for the most part it was an unhappy, guilt-ridden time, and we did not know what the future held.

She returned to Holland and I to Morocco. We continued to meet—in Paris, in Tangier, in Amsterdam—but the central question had not been answered. When it finally became clear to Madeleine that her husband and family would never give their consent to take Julie out of the country, she packed her suitcases for the last time and moved with me into the Petite Maison in Marrakesh.

*February 5, on the bus*
*(Montevideo, Uruguay-Porto Alegre, Brazil)*

Once more I am troubled by dreams. Non-stop, the whole night long, a succession of disturbing and semi-comprehensible images streamed through my head, as we sped along the highway. I had no clear idea of where I was, or even what country we might be in. Old childhood friends (although we may no longer recognize each other, our camaraderie is still fostered by my jealous subconscious). We were running and running, escaping in shiny black round automobiles. Cars '45-'46 vintage. (My father owned a 1946 black Ford sedan.) Rocked by the dream and rough roads I awoke in a sweat. Peering through the window at lights flashing by, illuminating cameo scenes of Latin roadhouses and all-night filling stations, I stared and barely comprehended before being gripped again by the heavy hand of the dream, yanking me back to sleep. The dream immediately recommenced, right where it left off. Once more I was pulled back through time . . . the lunatic race to escape, as the bus plunged on through the night.

Morning. Dixieland brought me to my senses. The stewardess poured me a shot. I stared blankly at the green flowing fields of Rio Grande do Sul, reminiscent of rural Georgia or Alabama. White flamingos. The tape switched to Glenn Miller, expanding my nostalgia for time past as we swung across the plains.

Porto Alegre came into sight across the unbroken greenery. Skyscrapers sat atop feathery bushes. High-risers balanced delicately on tree limbs and misty shrubbery. Green leaves gracefully gave lift to cement blocks.

*prio* = here I come
*maté* = Paraguay tea
*hammock* = Brazil bed

A rustic road house on the road to Rio. Raw whiskey, red wine, pink steak, black beans *(feijão)*, and the couscous-like manioc. Another collection of diversely formed and variously colored Brazilian travellers diverted my attention from the meal. The mixture of blonds and blacks—have we arrived in Germany, or have we crossed over to Africa? And, as in all of Latin America, bright-colored female toenails flashed across the floor. The music started up, and red blue pink yellow orange silver mauve gold and pearl lights kicked and swirled over the rough boards.

Getting drunk about now!

*February 6*

Another hectic night on the bus—a long-distance *letobus,* or bed bus serving whiskey, with reclining seats the size of barber-chairs. Another procession of semi-comprehensible dreams usurped my rest. I'm buying a piece of yellow cloth, with a red border. It's huge—the size of a football field. You could stitch a big top from it. As it lies upon the green sward, the wind ripples the cloth, creating moving bubbles like small animals running beneath. A crime has been committed. A child murdered and drowned in mud. Everybody knows that Pastora, the Paraguayan maid, a dark-haired girl of eighteen, did it . . . M and I return to Marrakesh. By chance we encounter Paul Bowles marching in a parade on a foggy street at night. (You rarely see fog in that Saigon of the Sahara.) Replying to his surprised queries, we proceed to tell him a pack of lies concerning the route of our return. We catch sight of the maid walking with others five abreast. We tail her, but she doesn't recognize us. M whispers loudly into her ear: "Pa—Past—Pastora! You did it!"

"Still, above all it was the very blankness and emptiness of the place that most appealed to (W. H.) Hudson, and he soon realized that observation was no longer a conscious mental undertaking, but a subconscious and mystical process of self-realization."

*Rio. February 7*
*Hotel California $85.00*

A brief, hurried letter from M with the news that her Uncle Daan has died. She doesn't want to hang around Holland much longer. She's already making plans to leave for Africa —her Africa, Swaziland, not mine. I better get back there, pronto. *"Sabes todo."*

In Brazil the radio news broadcasts are preceded and terminated by doom music, appropriate to the thickening of the plot in a horror story. A sinister voice announces the day's events.

When the photographs of "terrorists" confront me in the post office and other public places where they are prominently displayed, I see students, boys and girls with young faces and sad, soft eyes not unlike those of caged animals who inhabit the municipal zoo. Each has an identifying number and an endearing alias: "The Doll," "The Monkey," "Emanuelita," "Cigar," etc. And the older bearded ones look like professors to me. How did they get to be branded as "assassins," "anarchists," "arsonists"—wanted dead or alive? Copacabana. A gaudy display of smooth and muscular flesh on the beach. Breasts and buttocks willingly exposed, like prime beef on the hoof, but at what price? Quick movements on the burning sands indicate that the volleyball and soccer games have begun. I thought I knew something about body surfing, but nothing compared to the tricks the Rio boys pull in the big surf.

*February 8*

Dwarfs. Wherever and in whatever age they have been found, whether in Velázquez's canvasses or hustling travellers like me on the Copacabana, they all look alike. The same sad bright eyes, reflecting the same dwarf soul—the brotherhood of deformity.

Eyes switch with the speed of slot-machine plums. Smooth bellies. Sexual preoccupations persist, about which I do nothing. Might as well be concerned about the state of the world—can't do much about that, either.

Melville's pet tortoise, whose progress had seemed inexorable, collided with the mast of the ship upon which it sailed. However much it scratched the deck and heaved, for the tortoise it was the end of the line.

It's been two months since she laid a gentle hand on me. Inspecting the colorful Brazilian gemstones in Stern's jewelry showroom, I hope my selection of semi-precious stones might stir the affection I deeply miss. In how many seedy hotel rooms have I lain alone and loved . . .

The fragile, bird-like kites of Copacabana. The kids operate them. Above the tooting of horns, the crunch and rumble of thousands of polluting engines, and the herd of blubbery flesh heaving on the sand, the kites soar to great heights. Flimsily constructed, they fly best in a light breeze and often, after staying aloft for several minutes, plunge suddenly earthwards, for no apparent reason at all, while the expert kids, tugging and manoeuvring the long lines, usually succeed in arresting the precipitous descent before the kite touches earth. I like to watch them. The sight of the kites releases my mind from heavy preoccupations. I think of Frost's bender of birches. Ponderous by nature, man has nevertheless been able to launch his thoughts. Like these kites they quickly soar, needing little lift in the wafting breeze. But just as easily, unresponsive to all manner of tugs and jerks, they flutter back to earth, sometimes landing with a splintering crash. Dodging among blobs of pink flesh roasting under an oven sun, the kids dash through the thundering traffic to retrieve them. With the line rewound on a beer can, the fragile craft is relaunched, a tail of newspaper clippings attached to steady the ascent.

Teenage bodies daringly but blandly displayed. Pink breasts and dark faces. Where are their mothers and what do they think? Uh oh, here they come—fatigued flesh bulging over mini-bikinis. Bodies and more bodies. Volleyball and soccer—quick movements on the burning sand.

"I have found that bare feet take very kindly to the earth."
—W. H. Hudson

A boy, ten or eleven years old, elegantly attired, bare feet notwithstanding, in a conservative charcoal suit, clean white shirt and pink necktie, straight blond hair falling to his shoulders, entered the restaurant peddling roses from a basket. He laid a rose upon the tablecloth and took one step backward. The eyes and face gave nothing away. If, within a few seconds, the diner had not picked up the rose or made some sign that he would buy it, the boy retrieved it and proceeded to the next table. His mother waited by the door.

*February 9*

Copacabana beach at 7 o'clock in the morning. The early risers jog and do pushups. The ladies' exercise class, with much huffing and puffing, swings into action. The sunbathers, like soldiers preparing for a siege, heap up mounds of sand upon which to prostrate themselves before the flaming god which has only just risen from the sea. Despite these various activities, a calm pervades. The idle mob has not yet arrived. The sea is placid, unmarked by breezes, and the long swell rises up and expends itself with a gasp upon clean sand. This is the serious, quiet hour. These people have come to the beach with a sense of purpose, which the sea solemnly acknowledges.

You smell a lot of patchouli around Rio.

*February 10, Bahia. Hotel Plaza $97.00*
*Chez Suzanne (fish)*
*Churrascaria Carreta (meat)*

The same routine follows everywhere. Having arrived in a completely strange city, you go over the map with the concierge in your fancy hotel. Trying to get your bearings, you ask where is the liveliest part of town, where the action is. Intuitively, your finger wanders to the congested area near the port, where the streets radiate and wind round one another in a crazy spiderweb pattern. "Oh no!" the man nearly shouts, grimacing, as it were, from some stench your finger has released by merely touching the area. One cannot eat there, or drink, or hardly breathe. And he steers your finger to another quarter, where the streets are laid out in a neat grid, also where your hotel happens to be located. Later, trusting your original instinct, you make your way into the web and discover that cantinas have been set up in the street. The folks make music and dance all night.

A lateen sail departing under moonlight . . . ancient stone parapets. How they built, these Portuguese—the work of titans. The men who toiled here must have known the Moroccan ports where similar ramparts still stand—Tangier, Asilah, El Jadida, and Mogador. They sailed down the African coast before crossing the neck of the Atlantic to Brazil.
Scales of dead fish on the mosaic sidewalk glitter in the moonlight. Rank fish odor assaults the nostrils. Here in northeast South America the Atlantic smells different than the Pacific. The Atlantic smells of fruit and vegetable decay. It is a relaxed, tropical sea, while the Pacific thunders against the coastal desert and stirs up the dust, Andean dust—the pulverized bones of pelicans, seals, seagulls, and men. Pelican droppings bleach the jutting rocks. Cries of gulls split the muffled roar. The cold

Pacific belongs to the Indians. This hot Atlantic is an African sea. It belongs to the blacks, their coconuts and their palm trees, and their special odor.

Attracted by screeching noises late at night I entered a cobbler shop and discovered a flock of parrots living in shoes. They whistled and squawked at me.

Down on the beach, meanwhile, naked men were casting lines into the void. Mulatto sailors slept on their sail spread on the sand. Their bodies formed dark hieroglyphs against the milky white cloth. This town fills me with desire. I want to bed down on the beach and sail with them in the morning. I wish to accompany them to the fishing grounds and know where they harvest the coconuts. Desire, as usual, far advanced beyond any hope of realization. As usual I will have to travel and live with these lusty figures in my imagination.

*February 11*

The frenzied activity in the port on a Saturday morning. Ferry-boats depart, and the lateen-rigged sailboats, laden with fruit, manioc and squealing pigs, arrive from the islands. The black crew exhibits spectacular physiques and much good humor as they wrestle with the young animals. Yellow paint peels from the façades of the colonial edifices in the port, built to the order of the white man. I like to think that the decay of the town speaks of people who like things the way they are, like old clothes or comfortable homes they do not wish to change or repair. High rises going up apace, however, testify to a powerful sentiment that will not wait. I see a brutal sterility in those shiny towers.

At the *Jardím de Ala* (Garden of Allah). When I stepped from the taxi, a young fellow came forward with the bland assurance of a doorman. Taking my hand in his, he invited me to join him and his mates for a smoke in a grove of palms.

Classic tropical beaches out of a travel brochure. The water warm and clear, the best surfing I've ever had, with local enthusiasts not quite so show-offy as the Rio boys. Swimming out to catch the big rollers, I wondered about sharks. While riding the thundering herd, a black head popped up in front of me. I went right over him. He surfaced laughing, black skin gleaming as it streamed water, and said he'd said a quick Ave Maria when he saw me bearing down upon him. On leaving the sea, one must, if the skin is white, don a shirt and straw hat right away to avoid being broiled alive by the sun. The blacks labor all day bare-backed in it. They insert the mosaic sidewalk pieces and pound them down with great wooden mallets.

On the beach, rotund African ladies munching sugar cane and loaded with cowry-shell necklaces sell the most tasty goodies—fried corn meal stuffed with tiny shrimp and chips of fresh fish. Numerous fiery sauces. Ice-cold beer in snap-top cans. Boys wield deft machetes as they whack off the tops of chilled coconuts. What delight on that torrid strand! After you've sucked out the milk, they crack the hull for you, and you scrape out the jellyish white flesh with a sliver of husk. When I asked a woman selling matches and mangoes about the *Macumba*, or Brazilian voodoo, she opened the door to her shack, beckoned me inside, and showed me a candle flickering in a nest of feathers and leaves on the floor. The Macumbera's eyes wanted mine to look into them, but mine became afraid, a shiver ran through me, and my bird eyes flew quickly away. She was good-looking in an imperious way. The smile appealed, but the eyes spoke a different language.

No light in those oily eyes, the texture of which reminded me of snakeskin, shiny and creased.

For what purpose her eyes sought mine I cannot say. There was no invitation in that look, only an hypnotic insistence. My ingenuous inquiries about *Macumba* perhaps pricked her interest in the unsuspecting foreigner, perhaps whetted her appetite for an easy victim. *Macumba,* like all other rackets, games and systems, is all about power and money. No surprise the women are in control.

*February 12*

Caught by a sudden rainstorm at the Mercado Modelo, I checked my watch (12.05 PM) and decided to take a seat, eagerly offered by the young black waitresses, at one of the tables beneath the great rotunda. The massive wooden beams, strong enough to support a railroad (and having the appearance of a train trestle), were supported by bulbous stone columns, reminiscent of Karnak. Rice and beans, fish and *batida* (2)—a tasty mixture of rum and cashew juice—serenaded by a band of minstrels playing the *agogo* and *berimbau* (onomatopoeia), the one-stringed harp. An excellent hour.

A number of wild men patrol these streets—long beards, black skin, insane clothes—hippies from central Amazonia?
How the Brazilians love their coffee! One shot keeps you on your toes for an hour.

Pierre Verger, whom I have been looking for ever since I got here, the man I came to Bahia to see, bearing a letter of introduction from my friend Robert Gerofi in Tangier, I found waiting for me in the lobby of my hotel.

I had thought this breed of far-flung French intellectual had ceased to exist. Dressed in a loose white shirt , trousers (rather dirty) and sandals, he might have been taken for a 19th-century explorer, such as Brazza, or a 20th-century beachcomber or investigator, rather going to pieces in the tropics. A little of each, as it turned out—a man who has shed excess pieces of western consciousness in order to live in a practical and simple manner among the Brazilians.

He led me through the streets of the city he loves. Children ran up to him. He was continually saluted from all sides, especially by the blacks. We visited the Jesuit church with its walls of gold, passed along narrow streets prohibited to automobiles, admired a magnificent mango which, he told me, when threatened by the municipal authorities for blocking the sidewalk, was defended by its gardener with a rifle. The officials relented. We visited a Saturday fruit and veg market in the port, then took a taxi to his house in a quarter known as Villa America. I didn't know quite what to expect—a penthouse or a shack.

The latter. Located upon a hillside among cane and bananas in a poor black neighborhood. When we alighted from the taxi, cheerful salutations from all sides, which he took much delight in acknowledging. Not exactly a shack, but a small, modest and very simple house—loosely tiled roof with light showing through the chinks.

A sitting room/office in front—papers and books strewn about, the shelves loaded with a myriad of local objects. Bedroom— narrow unmade bed, a long bookshelf sagging beneath a library of white hand-cut books in French and Portuguese. Bathroom/kitchen and another darker room which he showed me later, pointing out his *candomblé* (local Voodoo word for shrine) in the corner, complete with flickering candle and the stylized double-edged axes from Brazil and Africa. This was Shongo's place. Shongo is an African god.

As we sipped *maté* flavoured with anise, he showed me his

photographs and books. Thick tomes dealing with the communication, flux and reflux, trade, and mutual influence between the black people of northeast Brazil and West Africa, published in Dakar and Paris. While he showered, I leafed through a book of photographs he took in the 1940's of the Andean Indians in Bolivia and Peru. Although the photos were poorly printed due to war shortages, they were unique. He had caught the oriental, high-altitude, almost extra-terrestrial quality of these peoples' lives and faces, especially their dances. This is a man of 70 years.

Later we caught a bus down the coast. (We stopped briefly at Rio Vermelho to buy cold cocos. When the bus pulled in, we threw down the cocos and ran for it.) The return trip, on a bus packed tighter than a slave ship, I found fatiguing and claustrophobic, but Pierre did not mind. He owns no car; he goes everywhere by bus or on foot. By the end of the day, I was worn out and grateful that I would not have to rise early the next day, Sunday. (Pierre would be up by 5 AM).

We had dinner Chez Suzanne, where he was saluted by waiters like a long-lost friend. The patron came and sat with us.

Pierre said he would like to erect a monument to the Portuguese slavers who brought the Africans to Bahia. I expressed standard horror to the idea. But, he went on, the blacks brought such vitality with them, their music, and their particular African spirit. Without them, Bahia would never have achieved its unique culture. Their gentleness—it is chiefly for this that Pierre says he lives in Bahia, as he has for the past 25 years.

After dinner we returned to the old center of town to attend a street celebration. *Capoeira,* a kind of harmless stylized karate dance performed to music (the participants are not supposed to make contact with their ballet-like leaps and kicks, although often they do), which terminated in hilarious confusion, the entire crowd getting into the act. As usual, Pierre was very well known, a local celebrity, acknowledging hails from all sides.

We went back via the red-light district, once the most fashionable part of town. Seventy years old, striding along the decrepit, noisy, degenerate street, at one time extremely elegant, which he hopes it will one day be again, once the crumbling town houses are restored, he delicately shed the not so delicate embraces of the aggressive night ladies.

Peering in through the open window of the restaurant, a slack-jawed idiot fixed his black cloudy eyes unblinkingly on my own. A large shrimp, transfixed upon my fork, hovered in mid-air. His eyes moved, unhurriedly, from me to the shrimp, then back to me; and we stared at each other for a few seconds before he shuffled away. A gaze like that, out of time and out of context, shakes one's confidence and diminishes the appetite.

*Candomblé (yesterday, Sunday)*

Tired out from tramping over the city, I rose late and went straight to the beach, where I rode the waves all morning. Returning to the hotel, I changed my clothes and ate a fish lunch Chez Suzanne (where the idiot spooked me with his dull eye). Took a bus to Itapaon and, savoring a coconut ice cream in the hot sun, waited by the sea. Long dugout fishing canoes were drawn up on the beach, draped with nets.

Pierre had gone out at 6 AM to participate in the sacrifice of a ram. If he hadn't appeared at Itapaon by 3.15 PM, my instructions were to take the microbus to Ipitanga, find the road to the beach where, when it rose beyond the last houses, I was to turn off to the left for 500 meters, and ask for the house of Balbino.

Pierre, however, turned up with friends in an automobile, and we drove to Ipitanga. We pulled off the road into a white sandy area, white sand of such purity I had to squint in the sunlight. Bright green shrubbery grew about—a shrub whose leaves, Pierre pointed out, are used in controlling the dancers in a state of trance. The bushes gave the place the appearance of a late spring snowfall, from which the dark shrubbery had quickly pushed.

We came to a group of wattle houses and found Balbino in his cool palm-frond hut, about 30 yards from the others. He is 32, looks 25, a young priest/prince, which he does not for a moment forget. Soon he will be departing for Africa. Turbanned and dressed in white, he was having his fingernails pared by a young initiate, also in white, who looked like a medical intern, with unexplained blood stains on his white gauze turban.

After exchanging greetings, in which Balbino exhibited a friendly indifference, we visited the central hut, where the *Candomblé* ceremony would take place. Wattle walls freshly whitewashed, loosely tiled roof, light in the chinks, mud floor layered over with white sand and sprinkled with tiny green leaves. To all entrances, both doors and windows, were attached "spirit brushes"—feathery cane- and palm-frond arrangements that reminded me of those Madeleine and I passed through to gain entrance to the Bushnegro villages along the Maroni River in Surinam. Three drums, each tied with a thick ribbon, were grouped on a small raised stage at one end. Next to these stood three mirror-backed chairs, one larger and throne-like, also bound with a fat cloth ribbon. The roof beams were festooned with sections of lacy cloth, red and white paper streamers, and fine palm fronds (*mari-wo*), as if the New Year were about to enter. The general impression was of cleanliness and freshness, with a cool breeze blowing through the window, moving the leaves. Almost antiseptic, hospital-like, it was a spot where human spirits can find wholeness and good health.

Returning to Balbino's hut, we found the intern covering his nails with clear polish. Another mat was found, and we stretched out. From the main hut came the sounds of the chief drummer (*alabé*, or owner of the gourd) warming his hands.

In another hut, the women were preparing long white wedding-like gowns, with much laughter and chat.

Coffee was served by another "intern" with a long chain of blue beads around his neck and a bell attached to his ankle. Pierre told me he is "for sale." Having just finished his initiation, he has acquired an African name and is waiting for a "godfather" to adopt him.

Across the way, the ladies were doing something with banana leaves and palm fronds. A handsome young woman swung a charcoal iron in a doorway . . . free female laughter tinkled from within.

Balbino has organized this *Candomblé*, a "holy mother" in Salvador having recently died, and her devotees, Balbino among them, having dispersed. Pierrre told me that this woman had the current minister of the navy under her influence, and had succeeded in placing ten members of her family in the ministry. Just as I suspected, this colorful and touching but sometimes dangerous game is all about power.

A cool breeze and a peaceful message from the drum. I discovered a single cowry shell sewn into the mat. It was hot. We dozed off.

Small bushes had been planted in the sand. To me they appeared frail and forlorn, but were expected to survive. Water is given twice a day.

From the heights of the snow-white dunes, the sea was visible, about a mile distant to the east. Laughing, half-naked bathers returned along the dirt road. At the airport, equidistant to the west, a Boeing silently (the wind being from another quarter) landed—a sleek capsule gleaming incongruously in a field of palms and white sand. As the fragile yellow balloon of the sun floated perilously earthwards, a breeze got up.

Thirty or so wattle huts nestled within the boundary of sand. No other habitations were visible in the surrounding palm forest. White flags, marking the modest shrines, flew here and there. One contained a large stuffed snake. All the dwellings were of similar wattle construction, some with palm frond roofs, others tile. There was water at the base of some dunes. A hole in the sand, wider and deeper but similar to what a child might dig at the beach, yields a yellowish-brown liquid. Toward sunset the ladies and "interns" came down with square tin cans. Among the huts, meanwhile, the girls were beginning to circulate, showing off their snow-white gowns. The wind changed, and the Boeing departed noisily, Rio-bound.

The god *"Exu" (Eshoo)* must be pacified. The drums began softly. Balbino directed every movement. He chanted. An old woman shuffled in a circle around a girl leaning over and pouring oil (to calm), *farinha* (manioc powder) and water into a gourd. Three times the woman took the gourd, emptied it outside, and re-entered backwards. The initiates doffed their turbans. Three girls (13-14 years or younger) and two boys all have had their heads shaved. Balbino, the old woman and the others, including Pierre, made many † signs in the sand, then touched one finger to the temple. The initiates and three other participants passed the entire ceremony in attitudes of base prostration, Moslem-style, with forehead resting on two fists, one on top of the other. In the end they all danced for a moment, then suddenly, oddly, undramatically, it was over. You got the impression of a simple church ceremony.

We went out. Dusk. White sand magically moonlit. Jet-propelled bats chased invisible flying bugs. A child cried, and flames flickered wearily in the shrines. We were "invited" to lay 10 cruzieros at the shrine of Shongo, 4th King of the Yoruba, who presided over dishes of crabs and meaty bones (which we would eat later), plates of okra and polished stones. We entered respectfully without shoes and, with the rattle of a gourd, deposited a bill. The god of smallpox, garbed in straw, sat to one side.

Moonlight: girls in long white dresses wandered leisurely across the sand, elegant and light-footed like the young debutantes they are.

Balbino donned a cap studded with cowry shells, reminding me of the ones the Gnaoua musicians in Marrakesh wear. The dance began. Twenty or so people moving slowly in a circle, more of a shuffle than a dance, with frequent pauses for rest. The old woman who had led the preliminary ceremony began to lurch in an unexpected way, as if the music had woken an animal imprisoned within that sack of old black skin, which was now probing and pushing for a way out. Balbino danced briefly, then retired to his chair near the drummers, and led the chanting. The leaves and white sand had been scuffed away by the dancers' feet, leaving a red circle. The women doffed turbans . . . the initiates prostrated themselves before the doorway . . . a dog wandered in . . . it was all quite casual. All wore straw necklaces. Those who had on sandals now kicked them off. The drums would not cease . . . much cross-marking on the floor. † † † Then, quite abruptly, I realized that the great moment was approaching. Balbino returned to the center of the floor. Eyes closed he began to vibrate and wobble. Great cheers as the others danced around him, supported him when it seemed he would fall. The drums reached a fierce new tempo. Beads flying, Balbino's gone, he was under the spell. A joyous event, cheers for the god, cheers for the entranced, he who has been taken, entered and overcome.

An interlude. Balbino disappears. The sand under the moonlight—a river of milk. Candles burning marked the holy places. The drummers adjusted their instruments. In came Balbino, dressed as Shongo, crowned, King of the Yoruba. Cries of joy and exultation over the ecstasy of the new king, who now, aided, eyes closed, ascended the throne. Now he danced so wildly that the kingly robes were in continual need of tightening. The old women moved forward. Two others, a man and a woman, began to jerk and wobble. Cheers. Balbino disappeared once more as the tempo quickened, lithe bodies gleaming with sweat. Back he came naked to the waist, a wiry black body, and performed a wild ecstatic dance, out of control but not. He embraced the others, rubbing his sweat across their brows. The effect was contagious, one after another began to totter and sway, then hypnotically entered the dance. Great joy at the trance, for the god had entered the person.

When it was all over, everybody frolicked about outside, childlike, with much giggling and laughter, chasing each other about. At the invitation of Balbino, we sat down to a meal of beans, meaty bones and okra. Gumbo, I told them, is the African word for okra. Pierre nodded.

*February 14, Back in Rio. Hotel Olinda $31.00*

And so, with love on St. Valentine's Day, this episode draws to a close. Here set down you will find the combat record between solitude and the urge—no, the thirst—to create. That these must be allies in the latter endeavor now seems less straightforward than I had first supposed; for solitude often, for me, boils down to the boredom of the interminable probability of self; and, when left to one's self, the world can quickly ebb away to a startling distance. But like the sea it always returns with a certain predictability. I am the landlubber who watches, in these strange countries at least, the ebb and flow of the teeming sea with both feet planted firmly on the shore. Wishing to go to sea? Desiring deep baptism, or primary religious experience, is more likely. I do not believe I have anything vital to report concerning either. Of the road, yes, but dust cannot slake a powerful thirst, only aggravate it. There are times when thirst must be aggravated.

You sure do smell a lot of patchouli around Rio. I have just bought a pair of monkey-tooth necklaces from one of the ambulatory vendors who patrol these all-night cafés.

I think the road has fatigued me, but I can say I look forward to the future. Madeleine and I have a rendez-vous in Amsterdam, and I'll take her back to our home in Marrakesh. Today I took my last bath in a warm sea . . . tomorrow, the plane to New York where, no doubt, ice floes cake the Hudson. Already I am missing the Balbinos and the Pierres and the warm-weather folk with their blithe nakedness and their rhythms. Soon, with the crisp cold air entering at dawn, I will awake with a start at the sound of a thud—an over-ripe coco falling heavily to earth.

# *Epilogue*

Madeleine and I met in Holland as planned. She had been with her Uncle Daan until the end, and had helped her Aunt Peggy with the funeral arrangements. Julie was still in France. Madeleine had not been able to see her because her husband had obtained a court order preventing visiting rights without his permission. So far he had not given it. She had been to a lawyer who was initiating divorce proceedings.

We eventually moved back into our house in the Marrakesh oasis, but as the proceedings dragged on her absences became frequent and prolonged. She was spending more time travelling around Europe than with me in Morocco. Loneliness in my own home was like a hard lump in the chest. It seemed I was incapable of holding her or making her happy. During the North African winter the cold penetrated to the bones. Green logs hissed on the fire. The oasis telephone was a maddening device. It was almost impossible to get in touch with her. I felt like disappearing into another violent landscape—the Sahara.

Never had my work gone so poorly. In spite of the fresh material I had brought back from South America, I was making little progress on the novel. I hated my loneliness because it was so unproductive. It acted as a brake on creativity, spitting out sparks of bitterness and remorse.

The status of the Petite Maison became uncertain. A rumor went around Marrakesh that the property might be expropriated by the Moroccan authorities. The new landlord, a French doctor, friendly at first, soon made no secret of the fact that he wanted to evict us from our little adobe house.

A letter arrived from one of Rosita Ferreyros' children in Lima. He apologized for not having written sooner, but didn't have my address. He said that his mother went to church every day to light a candle and say a prayer for me. He wanted to express his gratitude, from him and his entire family, for saving her life.

Finally Madeleine and I agreed to go our separate ways. I rented an apartment in Tangier, leaving her in the Petite Maison with most of its contents. Shortly afterwards she telephoned to say that during one of her absences the new landlord had sent his men to the house. They had thrown all our furniture and her belongings "like hay" into the yard, changed the locks and sealed the doors. Our faithful gardener Ahmed had retrieved her things and taken them to his village for safekeeping, but Madeleine was obliged to move into another house in Marrakesh.

She called me from time to time, usually with another piece of bad news. Her family home in Holland had burned down. Her ex-husband had been killed in a riding accident in France. Even so she had been unable to gain custody of her daughter.

I looked back on our relationship with regret and guilt. Madeleine abandoned her husband and daughter for me. The love letters I wrote to Kenya shattered that little family, leaving Julie to grow up without a mother or father. I was the instigator, and now the only thing left are memories, some recorded here.

The novel I had carried around South America finally got published under the title *The Flight of the Pelican*.

Over the years I gradually lost touch with Madeleine but through mutual friends learned that she had married a South African and had gone to live in Tanzania where she was in charge of a large house and was surrounded by animals. Each year she returned to Europe to see her friends who noticed the sores on her legs which she did not seem to take seriously or treat properly.

The news came that she had contracted an infection which the doctors in Africa were unable to cure. She arrived in Amsterdam with a large hole in the back of her neck and was taken to the hospital in Utrecht, near her family home, where she was diagnosed with streptococcal gangrene. The unchecked infection had caused severe necrosis in her legs. In its advanced state the disease was incurable, and she was given morphine to ease the pain during her last days. Her family and friends rallied round. Mercifully the gangrene left her face untouched, and she was lucid to the end, except during dreamy states brought on by the drug. Julie visited, but there was never a reconciliation between mother and daughter. Julie declared Madeleine to be her biological mother, nothing more. Madeleine died in July, 1991, a few months before her fiftieth birthday.

Photo © by Joe McPhillips

## About the Author

After extensive travel in South America and graduation from Princeton University, John Hopkins lived for two decades in Tangier and Marrakesh, Morocco, where he found his vocation as a novelist among the company of such luminaries as Paul and Jane Bowles and William Burroughs.

Throughout all those years he has been an assiduous diarist.

Cadmus Editions published his *Tangier Diaries, 1962-1979,* in 1998.

The diary for his second voyage to South America, this time with Madeleine van Breugel, chronicling an imperfect love, was not included in *The Tangier Diaries, 1962-1979* and is presented here, thus completing publication of his diaries for that extended period.

John Hopkins now lives with his family in Oxfordshire in a National Trust house reserved for an American writer.

This
first Ameri-
can edition of *The
South American Diaries* printed
for Cadmus Editions by McNaughton &
Gunn in February 2008, consists of a trade
edition in wrappers and 76 signed copies
handbound in boards, 50 numbered
and 26 lettered. Composed and set
in Linotype-Hell Guardi, Heidel
berger Druckmaschinen AG
Linotype Library GmbH
Linocut /scratchboard
cover illustration by
Colleen Dwire
Map by Mynott
Design by
Jeffrey
Mill-
er